MW00380578

# The Complete KETO For Two Cookbook For Beginners 2019

*Linda Wade*



**Warning-Disclaimer**

The aim of the information in this book is to be as accurate as possible. However it is for informational purposes only and comes with no guarantees. The author and publisher shall have neither liability or responsibility to anyone with respect to any loss or damage caused, or alleged to be caused, directly or indirectly by the information provided in this book.

All product and company names used in this book are Trademarks™ or Registered® Trademarks of their respective holders. Their use in this book does not imply any affiliation with or endorsement by them. All trademarks and brand names used in this book are for clarifying purposes only.

# Contents

# My Keto Journey

My weight-loss journey began 2 years ago, a few months before my wedding day. I've been overweight all my life but I never thought too much about my appearance, fashionable clothes, and beauty standards. Moreover, I never weighed myself. Growing up, I realized that I am not naturally thin, but I am smart enough to learn how to love my body regardless of a socially preferred image. Unfortunately, I only learned to make excuses for my unhealthy weight such as "I've always been overweight" or "Beauty trends are constantly changing and they are actually wrong." "I deserve this chocolate cake. Life is too short." There were so many diet-derailing excuses in my life and I just kept busy with school activities. In reality, I had wrong beliefs and never had a strong motivation to make a change in my life. One day, I went to a plus size bridal shop to try on some wedding dresses. I was embarrassed and frustrated in a fitting room because I just realized how big I'd got! I decided – that's enough, I don't want any more excuses, I am going to lose weight and become happy! I tried many different dietary programs throughout the whole year but nothing special has happened. I lost a few pounds and I gained them all back.

One day, I discovered a nutrition plan that includes plenty of fat, a certain amount of protein and zero to low-carb foods. Does it mean weight loss without dieting? Come on! I was very skeptical! On the other hand, that intrigued me and I decided to read articles and studies about the ketogenic lifestyle; after that, I decided to give it a try, it costs me nothing. Voilà! I did it! I lost six pounds in the first month. In the same time, I started cooking regularly for me and my husband and that's where I found inspiration for this cookbook.

When I started keeping track of my calories and carb intake, focusing on lean proteins, and was exercising regularly five times a week, my weight-loss journey began! I started losing 1 to 2 pounds per week, gradually and steadily. Once I achieved my goal weight, I could afford some extra carbs or calories but I tried to rotate low-carb days with moderate-carb and high-carb days. This nutrition strategy is also known as cyclic ketogenic diet and it actually works for me, so I warmly recommend it. Health, happiness, and healthy BMI are not just about a diet regimen or meal plan. This is my ongoing lifestyle with new eating and exercise habits. A good dietary regimen can revitalize your health, boost your metabolism and speed up your weight loss. I finally realized: you do not have to follow trends blindly but it's worth making an effort to change bad eating habits as well as look your best and feel your best.

Are you looking for keto recipes that are adjusted for only two servings? Do you need creative and delicious recipes for one of the most popular diets in the world? Well, you are in the right place. This recipe collection will take home-cooked meals up a notch! I've been collecting recipes for at least 5 years and I succeeded to adapt most of them to fit my new keto lifestyle. All 75 recipes come from home cooks – my grandma, my neighbor, and my mom. This collection actually covers both traditional and trendy recipes so your partner won't resist a bowl of warming keto soup or a piece of delectable keto cheesecake.

# What is so Fascinating about Ketogenic Diet?

A ketogenic diet is a low-carb, high-fat and adequate-protein dietary regimen. During this eating plan, your body produces less glucose and more ketones; consequently, it uses ketones as energy or fuel for its normal activities. Ketosis is a natural process so after you have been on the ketogenic diet for 7 to 8 days, your body simply gets used to it. Your body and your brain start using ketones to fuel energy. Scientists founded a low number of ketones in the blood after overnight fasting too. In this way, you can lose weight and improve your physical health and mental performances. Besides being effective in promoting weight loss, cutting out carbs can lower insulin and blood sugar levels. This nutrition plan may play a role in the prevention of common diseases, including metabolic syndrome, type 2 bipolar disorder, Parkinson's disease, and certain cancers. If you're curious, a keto diet could be worth considering!

Basically, you should eat high-quality protein foods such as fish, poultry, and eggs, full-fat dairy products, and whole food such as nuts, seeds, and vegetables. However, not everything is black and white, there are foods that get the big thumbs down. You should avoid grains, rice, legumes, and starchy fruits. You will be on extremely low carb content, moderate amounts of protein and high-fat content. How does that sound to you? Well, losing pounds and eliminating hunger, while eating big portions of fatty and high-protein foods sounds like a dream come true to me.

When it comes to the keto diet macros, there is not one plan with a specific ratio of macronutrients. However, experts suggest 5% carbs, 20% protein, and 75% fats from total daily calories and I stick to this formula. I also suggest trying to stay within your calorie needs. Most ketoers and nutritionists claim that you do not have to count calories on a low carb-diet. I just want to play it safe and track my calorie intake. It can drastically speed up your weight loss. Once you get used to it, counting calories and macros is easy and fun. On the keto diet, you can also expect the appetite suppression so you won't need too many calories. On the other hand, ketosis may boost the body's metabolism. A related point to consider is a calorie deficit. Although lower calorie intake is necessary for weight loss, if it dips too low, it could be counterproductive! Big calorie deficit could actually slow down your metabolism. Moreover, you should eat high-quality fat to burn fat on the ketogenic diet.

**Here's what you should eat:**

Meat – pork, beef, veal, lamb, and goat,

Poultry – chicken, turkey, duck, and goose.

Fish & Seafood – fat fish, white fish, shrimp, sea scallops, lobster, mussels, clams, oysters, crab, and squid.

Dairy products –full-fat sour cream, Greek-style yoghurt, cheese, heavy whipping cream, and double cream.

Eggs – hard-boiled, fried, poached, and scrambled.

Vegetables – asparagus, onion, garlic, cauliflower broccoli, cucumber, Brussels sprouts, zucchini, and tomatoes. If you consume pickled vegetables pay attention to added sugar.

Nuts – pecans, Brazil nuts, coconut, macadamia nuts, walnuts, hazelnuts, pine nuts, almonds and peanuts. You can eat unsweetened nut butter as well. Opt for homemade versions and you can't go wrong.

Seeds – flax seeds, chia seeds, sesame seeds, and sunflower seeds. You can also eat tahini (sesame paste) and other types of seed butters.

Fats – olive oil, coconut oil, butter, ghee, and avocado.

Fruits – keto friendly fruit options include berries, lemon, lime, and melon.

Herbs and spices (fresh or dried); bouillon cubes and granules.

Sauces & Condiments – tomato sauce, vinegar, hot sauce, mustard, and mayonnaise.

Canned food: sauerkraut, pickles, tomatoes, and olives (no added sugar).

Baking ingredients: almond flour, coconut flour, baking powder, baking soda, sugar-free chocolate, and cocoa powder.

Alcoholic beverages: Whiskey, brandy, rum, vodka, and tequila, and dry martini.

Vegetarian protein sources – tofu, tempeh, nutritional yeast, coconut yogurt, unsweetened dairy-free milk, Shirataki noodles, and seaweed (spirulina, chlorella, nori, kelp, and wakame).

Drink options include coffee, tea, diet soda, keto smoothies, zero carb energy drinks, sparkling water, and seltzer.
Keto sweeteners: Monk fruit and Stevia are zero-carb sweeteners; Splenda contains 0.5 grams of carbs per 1 gram while Erythritol and Xylitol both contain 4 grams of carbs per 1 teaspoon.

**What should be avoided on the ketogenic diet?**
Common types of flours including bread flour, all-purpose flour, cake flour, cornmeal, and arrowroot.
Legumes: Beans, lentils, and dried peas.
Grains & pseudo-cereals such as rice (white, brown, wild), millet, corn, quinoa, amaranth, oats, barley, and buckwheat.
Starchy vegetables and fruits such as potatoes, yams, root veggies, mesquite, banana, plantain, and tapioca.
Trans fats and hydrogenated oil: vegetable shortening, corn oil, cottonseed oil, soybean oil, and margarine. You can find hydrogenated oils in packaged foods so try to cook your meals from scratch instead of relying on boxed versions.
Sugars – granulated sugar (white and brown), muscovado sugar, powdered sugar, honey, maple syrup, molasses, agave nectar, carob syrup, sorghum syrup, corn syrup, rice syrup, malt syrup, barley malt, panocha, scant, treacle, and cane juice.
Sugary drinks: sodas and energy drinks.
Almost all types of fruits including fresh, dried, and canned fruits.

In addition to these foods, limit packaged foods, premade baked foods, ready-to-use dough, coffee creamers (dairy and nondairy), fried foods, and packaged snacks. You can print a list of keto diet foods and bring it with you to the grocery store. When it comes to the grocery shopping, always check the labels for hidden added sugars. Throw out or donate carbohydrate-rich foods to properly organize your keto pantry.

# Benefits of the Ketogenic Diet

1. **Sustained energy.** On ketosis, your body breaks down fat instead of carbs. Eating healthy fats is the key to increased energy. Healthy fats (e.g. avocado, nuts, seeds, coconut oil) which are monounsaturated fat and polyunsaturated fats can increase good cholesterol (HDL High-density lipoprotein). In this way, your body is forced to run on fat. Make sure to limit your saturated fat intake and avoid trans fats at all costs. Trans fats are hydrogenated oils and you can find them in margarine, fried fast foods, doughnuts, cookies, cakes and packaged foods.

2. **Heart health.** Monounsaturated and polyunsaturated fats can lower your risk for heart disease. These healthy fats contain omega-3 fatty acids that can reduce triglyceride levels, lower blood pressure, and decrease irregular heartbeats. You should eat shrimp, mackerel, salmon, seabass, sardines, and other types of fatty fish. For vegetarians, opt for seaweed, algae, flax seeds, hemp seeds, walnuts, chia seeds, and edamame.

3. **Mental clarity and focus.** On a keto diet, your brain uses ketones as the main source of energy; consequently, the level of toxins drops significantly. It can improve your focus, concentration and mental health. The ketogenic diet has been proven effective in controlling epilepsy and preventing several neurological disorders.

4. **Healthy eating habits.** A keto diet promotes natural, whole and minimally processed foods. Eat real foods such as fresh vegetables, all-natural and wild-caught fish, pasture-raised eggs, and organic products. And go organic whenever possible!

5. **Weight loss and maintaining an ideal weight.**

   Obesity is not just an aesthetic issue; actually, the American Medical Association recognizes obesity as a disease. Overweight people are more likely to suffer from heart disease, high blood pressure, diabetes, metabolic syndrome, and cancer.

My journey was filled with highs and lows. At first, you may not feel great and enthusiastic since you may have symptoms of the keto flu. Weakness, headache, bad taste in the mouth, and constipation are normal reactions but it does not have to be that way. I didn't have any of those symptoms. First things first, I had to heal my relationship with food. I became aware that I used to eat for emotional reasons in many circumstances: to cope with stress, to reward myself, to punish myself. I found comfort in food! My primary goal was to found the answers. I read tons of articles and testimonials and I finally realized: It is not about food! Everything happens unconsciously, emotional eating is my way to find temporary relief from difficult feelings and stressful situations. I should stop hating my body! There is more than one cause of weight gain, including genetic predisposition, and hormonal imbalance, high insulin levels. Improving your metabolic processes does not happen overnight. It took me about six weeks to benefit from a keto diet. Nature does not hurry, so be patient!

As I mentioned before, I maintain my healthy weight by practicing a carb cycling diet plan. How does it work in practice? You should simply rotate moderate carb, low carb, no carb, and high carb days throughout the week; further, you should consume a certain amount of protein; and last but not least, your fat intake is inversely proportional to the carb intake. Your daily activities also count – you should consume moderate to high amounts of carbs on days with high activity. For high carb days, consume 2-2.5 grams of carbs, 1 gram of protein and 0-0.1 grams of fat per pound bodyweight. As for moderate carb days, consume 1.5 grams of carbs, 1-1.2 grams of protein and 0.2 grams of fat per pound bodyweight. As for low carb days, consume 0.5 grams of carbs, 1.5 grams of protein and 0.35 grams of fat. You can also use an app to track macronutrient intake. Besides being good for weight loss, the carb cycling can improve insulin sensitivity (your body will respond better to carbs) as well as stimulate fat oxidization.

In addition to the carb cycling, small, manageable changes help rev up metabolic processes in my body. I try mindful eating and I do simple exercises to gain strength and muscles. Further, I never skip my breakfast, since skipping meals can slow down metabolism. Good keto breakfast can kick-start your metabolism, improve concentration, and maintain your energy levels throughout the day. Your body needs vitamins and nutrients in the morning. Moreover, if you do not eat breakfast, you will be hungry before lunchtime and you tend to snack more on sugary foods. Once you reached your ideal weight, eat more food for weight maintenance. Increase protein intake and add more carbohydrates only before and after workouts. Do not raise your daily carb intake suddenly; go slowly and let your body adapt to your new eating habits.

Paleo foods, nutrient-dense, whole and fiber-rich foods are great choices during this phase. Drink green tea and apple cider vinegar to maintain your weight. Other weight-loss friendly foods include chili peppers, eggs, lean beef, tuna, cottage cheese, chia seeds, coconut oil, and spices. A pro tip: eat protein with every meal!

I believe that your brain can be one of the biggest diet saboteurs. Afterwards, many studies have proven that our brain is key to treating obesity and eating disorders. Tiredness, boredom or dehydration can cause the brain to feel confused and make us think we are hungry even when we're not. To avoid this confusion, always have a healthy snack like fat bombs or keto bars on hand and be mindful of how much you're eating. Some other tricks include drinking coffee in the morning (it can speed up your calorie burn by 12%), drinking a glass of water before every meal, eating a salad and water-rich foods, planning your meals, and eating dessert occasionally. And last but not least, the best tip of all times – eat before grocery shopping!

In my opinion, a low-carb regimen will make you feel amazing in your body! Future researches may reveal more potential health benefits of low car diets, including metabolic syndrome, Alzheimer's and Parkinson's disease as well as several brain disorders.

## My Favorite Keto Substitutes

Are you struggling to find keto alternatives to your favorite rice and grain-based dishes? Luckily, here are my favorite replacements for common, high-carb foods that make my nutrition plan much better and my everyday routine much easier. I hope I've got you covered with these great low carb swaps!

<u>Sandwich buns</u> – what I miss the most is a big, mouth-watering, gourmet sandwich with crunchy ciabatta or soft dinner roll. You can trick yourself and your brain with low carb rolls, steamed egg buns, or grilled portobello mushrooms. I've recently discovered a great recipe for cheese buns. For two servings, you will need 1/2 cup shredded cheese such as cheddar, 4 tablespoons of hard cheese such as grated parmesan, and one egg. Bake at 375 degrees F until they have fully melted with a golden-brown crust.

Wraps – if you love tortilla or Greek pita, you can make them with almond flour that is mixed with chia or flax meal. Add an egg and you are good to go! Some creative ideas include lettuce leaves, Napa or Chinese cabbage, kale, cheese taco shells, thin slices of turkey breast, and so on.

Chips – why settle for ordinary potato chips when you can have so many alternatives. There are a lot of great ideas such as veggie chips, pork rinds, zucchini chips, green bean fries, kale chips, cheese chips, baked veggie sticks, and baked pickles. Pepperoni chips is a real game changer –simply microwave pepperoni slices on a piece of kitchen paper for 45 to 60 seconds or bake them in your oven until crispy about 10 to 15 minutes.

Pasta – some great alternatives include zoodles, veggie noodle (voodles), kelp noodles, and spaghetti squash. Using a spiralizing machine, you can turn cucumber, pumpkin or zucchini into noodle shapes and serve them with your favorite keto sauce. You can melt 1 cup of mozzarella cheese and mix it with 1 egg yolk; roll the "dough" until it is 1/8-inch thick; refrigerate for 6 to 7 hours; afterwards, bring a pot of water to boil and cook your "pasta" approximately 1 minute. I like to serve this pasta with spicy tomato sauce. What a brilliant idea!

Bread – you can use eggplant rounds, cloud bread (made of eggs and cream cheese), and nori sheets. Psyllium husk powder, with its whole-wheat texture and flavor, is a great ingredient for creating keto bread and cakes.

Bread products – cauliflower pizza crust, almond or coconut flour pancakes, zucchini lasagna, and eggplant lasagna.

Pancakes – prepare almond flour pancakes and you can save even 20 grams of carbs in one serving! You can also use coconut flour, walnut meal, pumpkin seed meal, and ground flax meal. Pro tip: if you have an allergic reaction to eggs, simply mix 1 tablespoon of flaxseeds with two tablespoons of water and let the mixture swell; you will have a great egg-like texture.

Bread crumbs – you can use pork rinds, psyllium husk, almond flour or coconut flour. They make a great coating for chicken nuggets or vegetable fritters.

Mashed potatoes – try mashed cauliflower or broccoli. Use butter and full-fat milk to make it smooth and delicious!

Rice – if you can't live without rice, you can replace ordinary white rice and grains with cauliflower rice, butternut squash rice, rutabaga rice or shirataki rice. They are the perfect substitute in common meals such as casseroles and paellas. They are especially delicious in combination with Indian food. These substitutes will not taste and look exactly like rice, but they will trick your stomach into feeling fool and keep you in ketosis.

Other keto substitutes – if you want to make hash browns, simply use spaghetti squash instead of potatoes. You will save 18 grams of carbs per serving! As for porridge and granola, you can make them with nuts and seeds (whole and ground). I also love flax crackers, fat bombs, and keto sushi (sashimi + cauliflower rice wrapped in cucumber slices).

## Home-Cooked Meals and How to Cook for Two

There are a lot of benefits of cooking at home.

**It can help promote your mental and physical health.** Although cooking for two may seem like a daunting task, it has a lot of health benefits. Commercially prepared foods are usually high in trans fats, partially hydrogenated oil, and sugar. These foods may contain some ingredients that could be dangerous if you have allergies and sensitivities. When you prepare your own meals, you are able to pay attention to hygiene and food safety. Use paper towels to reduce the risk of salmonella, always check your food with a food thermometer and make sure to wash your hands carefully before preparing meals. When we prepare our own food, we know exactly which ingredients are going into our food. We can use organic and non-GMO food and be sure of its quality. Cooking your own food enables you to create a well-balanced and healthy ketogenic diet for you and your beloved one. If you follow a specific diet plan such as ketogenic diet, tracking your nutrient intake is a must. Thus, eating poor quality restaurant food and fast food is absolutely out of the question. Cooking at home is the best option so that you only need a good cookbook and the will to succeed. Nailing a new recipe is a great experience! I love that feeling! Moreover, shopping locally and minimizing waste can be good for your community and healthier for the planet.

**Portion control.** It is another obvious benefit of eating at home. Restaurant meals are usually bigger than necessary. When you're cooking for two, use smaller cookware such as ceramic ramekins, mini pans, and small cupcake molds.

**It is a great opportunity for family time.** You can eat meals alone once in a while, but experts recommend that eating together can improve mental health. Many studies have found that people who regularly eat home-cooked meals are more likely to meet general nutrition recommendations. Did you know that couples that love to get into the kitchen together are happier and healthier?

**Meal planning.** In today's fast-paced world, you need a good diet plan that can keep up with your pace. You also need flavor-packed meals that are quick and easy to prepare. In this collection, I walk you through 75 easy-to follow keto recipes. These recipes will simplify your cooking routine since they contain ingredients that are available everywhere. Do not underestimate the planning part and you'll save a lot of time and money in the long run. Planning ahead can help you to avoid impulse buying.

If you cook for two, you can still buy in bulk. The key to cooking in bulk for two is to only buy what you can use up. You can always freeze extra food for later. Use your freezer to extend the life of perishable ingredients. You can even store bacon or butter cubes in your freezer and use just a few slices at a time. Baked goods can freeze beautifully as well. You can buy a whole package of meat on sale; to prevent freezer burn, wrap individual portions in your freezer.

**Cooking at home can save money.** Eating your own meals is usually cheaper than eating at a restaurant. Further, you can plan your daily and weekly menu and buy food in bulk; then, you can meal prep and cook in bulk so you can freeze leftovers. Follow detailed instructions in this recipe collection and you will spend less time in the kitchen and more time with your beloved one. With detailed nutritional analysis and 3-week meal plan, it can help you save your precious time and stay on track. Instead of cooking a 9×13 casserole, you can make two smaller dishes. Bake the first one to eat immediately and freeze the second one for later. On another day, when you are in a hurry, you can thaw you casserole and bake it. When you're cooking for two, bouillon concentrates and dried herbs can be used in many recipes, reducing your food waste. I often use frozen fruits and vegetables for smoothies, soups and stews; you do not have to thaw an entire bag. Get creative with your leftovers and make salads, sandwiches and fajitas!

Here are simple steps to begin your daily cooking habit:

**Take the first step towards change.** In fact, starting is the hardest part of anything but that doesn't mean you have to give up your diet and rely on takeout. If you are persistent, you can turn cooking into a habit. Once you get the hang of it, you can come up with your own creations.

**Focus on simple recipes.** If you are short on time, stop forcing yourself to prepare a three-course meal every night! You can try 1 to 2 complicated recipes per week, but the rest are easy meals that can be thrown together in less than 20 minutes.

**Accept not doing everything perfectly.** Mistakes are a part of being human. There are a few simple techniques that I use to become a better cook. It is important to keep your kitchen clean and tidy and organize your cabinets so the things are easily accessible. Do not overfill a pan and do not stir your food too much if you want crispy and flavorful vegetables or that golden, delicious crust on meat; otherwise, your food would turn out mushy and tasteless. Acidic foods (like lemon juice or tomatoes) and reactive pans (like aluminum) do not go hand in hand and you will end up with an unpleasant taste of your entire dish. When you're making a batter for baking, too much mixing may ruin your best recipe. When you're cooking pasta, always add salt to the water or you will end up with bland, dull pasta. Burnt or overcooked garlic can add an unpleasant taste to your dish. I learned it the hard way – overcooked garlic is gross. When stored in the refrigerator, onions, garlic, tomatoes, potatoes, zucchini, and tropical fruits lose their freshness faster than usual. And last but not least, the top chefs claim that a well-preheated pan is half success.

**Make the time for yourself.** I've been thinking – I am so good at scheduling of tasks for work and everyone else, but for myself... Making time for yourself is healthy and you'll be more productive in the long run. Start with one hour on Sunday and increase your time in the kitchen gradually.

**Create a list of must-have items.** Go shopping and stock your kitchen with low carb staples. Do not forget to add nuts, seeds, almond meal, olive oil, coconut oil, eggs, and non-starchy veggies to your list.

Home-cooked meals are certainly great, but there are days when you can't babysit the stove. Sometimes we can't stick to our schedule. In those days, simply use canned fish, chicken leftovers or raw vegetables to make satisfying meals and eat them for lunch and dinner. Consider cooking one-pot meals such as stews and soups, it can be a real game changer.

## A Few Words about Our Recipe Collection

This recipe collection will help you to avoid the "there's-nothing-to-eat" problem. From soups and sides to desserts, you will find a huge inspiration to cook at home and stick to your diet. To make this collection simple to use, I have selected the dishes according to food group, so you can easily search for a certain dish. If you are searching for fail-proof keto recipes that your spouse won't be able to resist, check this collection out. Every recipe contains the estimate cook time, the ingredients list, detailed directions, and nutritional analyses of macronutrients (protein, fat, carbs), sugar, and fiber. If you are new to the ketogenic diet, start with simple and familiar recipes such as chicken soup or beef stew. No matter how slow you go, it is important to keep moving towards your goal to be healthy and happy!

I also created an easy-to-follow 3-week plan that will help you to kick-start your keto adventure. You will explore the best keto recipes, from timeless old-fashioned recipes to innovative and creative delicacies. If you feel overwhelmed by the vast amount of dietary information, I am here to tell you that you will succeed. If I can do it, you can too! And remember whatever you are going through, never give up on yourself. This cookbook is ready to be your reliable companion guide that can make your diet even more achievable. Wish you the best of luck on your keto journey!

# 21-Day Meal Plan

This is a sample menu for three weeks on a ketogenic diet plan.

DAY 1
**Breakfast** – Omelet with Vegetables and Mexican Cotija Cheese
**Snack** – Caribbean-Style Chicken Wings
**Lunch** – Zucchini and Mushroom Lasagna; 1 handful of iceberg lettuce
**Dinner** – Asian-Style Fish Salad

DAY 2
**Breakfast** – 1 hard-boiled egg; 1 slice of bacon; 1 shake with 1/2 cup of coconut milk and protein powder
**Lunch** – Breakfast Keto Muffins; 1 serving of cauliflower rice
**Dinner** – Skillet Shrimp and Sea Scallop with Scallions; 1 medium tomato
**Dessert** – Chocolate and Coconut Fudge Brownies

DAY 3
**Breakfast** – Homemade Fluffy Tortillas with Cheese
**Lunch** – Saucy Cod with Mustard Greens
**Snack** – Ranch Kale Chips
**Dinner** – Easy Spicy Meatballs; 1 keto dinner roll

DAY 4
**Breakfast** – Omelet with veggies; 1 slice of bacon
**Lunch** – Pork Cutlets with Spanish Onion; 1 serving of coleslaw
**Dinner** – Roasted Old Bay Prawns
**Dessert** – Classic Blueberry Cheesecake

DAY 5
**Breakfast** – Classic Egg Salad
**Snack** – Zucchini Parmesan Chips
**Lunch** – Rich Winter Beef Stew; 1 handful of mixed green salad with a few drizzles of a freshly squeezed lemon juice
**Dinner** – Easy Baked Halibut Steaks; 1 teaspoon of mustard

DAY 6

**Breakfast** – Italian-Style Keto Sandwiches

**Lunch** – Melt-in-Your-Mouth Pork Roast; 1 serving of cauliflower rice

**Dinner** – Easy Zoodles with Sauce and Parmesan

**Dessert** – Creamy Almond Bars

DAY 7

**Breakfast** – Frittata with Kale and Cheese

**Lunch** – Easy Creamy Broccoli Soup; 1 large tomato; 1 cup of fried mushrooms with 1 tablespoon of butter

**Dinner** – Cheesy Zucchini Fritters

DAY 8

**Breakfast** – Scrambled eggs; 1 tomato; 1/2 cup of Greek-style yogurt

**Lunch** – Greek-Style Chicken Mélange; 1 serving of cauliflower rice

**Dinner** – Indian Cabbage Stir-Fry

**Dessert** – Chocolate Chip Blondies

DAY 9

**Breakfast** – Breakfast Keto Muffins; 1/2 cup of unsweetened almond milk

**Lunch** – Easiest Fish Jambalaya Ever; 1 serving of cabbage salad

**Dinner** – Spicy Glazed Eggplant; Pulled Pork with Mint and Cheese

DAY 10

**Breakfast** – Bell Pepper Boats

**Snack** – Greek-Style Pork Skewers with Sauce

**Lunch** – Authentic Thai Tom Kha Soup; 1/2 chicken breast; 1 scallion; 1/2 tomato

**Dinner** – Roasted Globe Artichokes with Cheese; a dollop of sour cream; 2 tablespoons tomato paste

DAY 11

**Breakfast** – 1 tablespoon of peanut butter; 1 slice of keto bread

**Lunch** – Cheese and Bacon Stuffed Chicken; 1 serving of cabbage salad

**Dinner** – Sea Bass with Vegetables and Dill Sauce

DAY 12

**Breakfast** – Spicy Masala and Brown Mushroom Omelet

**Snack** – Tender Ribs with Hot Sauce

**Lunch** – Pork Medallions with Cabbage; 1 serving of low-carb grilled vegetables

**Dinner** – Beef Teriyaki Skillet; 1/2 cup of full-fat Greek yogurt

DAY 13

**Breakfast** – Cauliflower Bites with Asiago Cheese

**Lunch** – Keto Tabbouleh Salad; Pork Loin Steaks in Creamy Pepper Sauce

**Dinner** – Favorite Chocolate Crepes

DAY 14

**Breakfast** – Double Cheese Baked Stuffed Peppers

**Lunch** – Sunday Roast Beef with Herbs; 1 handful of baby spinach with 1 teaspoon of mustard and 1 teaspoon of olive oil

**Dinner** – Caprese Asparagus Salad

**Dessert** – Pecan Pie Chocolate Truffles

DAY 15

**Breakfast** – Scrambled eggs; 1 tomato; 1/2 cup of Greek-style yogurt

**Lunch** – Warming Turkey and Leek Soup; 1 serving of roasted keto veggies

**Dinner** – Pulled Pork with Mint and Cheese; Spanish Ensalada de Pimientos Rojos

DAY 16

**Breakfast** – 2 hard-boiled eggs; 1/2 cup of Greek-style yogurt

**Lunch** – Mom's Festive Meatloaf

**Dinner** – Hungarian Fish Paprikash (Halászlé); Flourless Almond Butter Cookies

**Dessert** – Classic Chocolate Mousse

DAY 17

**Breakfast** – 2 hard-boiled eggs; 2 slices of Cheddar cheese

**Lunch** – Swiss Cheese Soup; Grilled Turkey Drumsticks; 1 fresh bell pepper

**Dinner** – Mini Meatloaves with Spinach; 1 cucumber

DAY 18

**Breakfast** – Nutty Cheesecakes Bowls

**Lunch** – Authentic Thai Tom Kha Soup; 1/2 grilled chicken breast

**Dinner** – Traditional Turkish Chicken Kebabs

DAY 19

**Breakfast** – Sunday Chicken Bake

**Lunch** – Rich and Easy Pork Ragout; 1 serving of steamed broccoli; 1 cucumber

**Dinner** – Sticky Barbecued Ribs; Broccoli Slaw with Tahini Dressing

**Dessert** – Chocolate and Coconut Fudge Brownies

DAY 20

**Breakfast** – Mediterranean Cauliflower Quiche with Cheese; 1 medium tomato with 2-3 Kalamata olives

**Lunch** – Beef and Garden Vegetable Soup; Roasted Portobellos with Edam and Herbs; 1 dollop of sour cream

**Snack** – Chunky Burger Dip

**Dinner** – Spring Duck Goulash

DAY 21

**Breakfast** –1 hard-boiled egg; 1 slice of bacon; 1 serving of blue cheese

**Lunch** – Mexican-Style Beef Casserole; 1 serving of cabbage salad

**Snack** – Skinny Cocktail Meatballs

**Dinner** – Chunky Pork Soup with Mustard Greens; Italian-Style Stuffed Peppers

# VEGETABLES & SIDE DISHES

2 Servings 45 minutes

# 1. Roasted Portobellos with Edam and Herbs

## Ingredients

- 2 tablespoons ghee, melted
- 1 pound white portobello mushrooms, cleaned and sliced
- 1/4 teaspoon smoked paprika
- 1/2 teaspoon cayenne pepper
- 1/4 teaspoon black pepper, cracked
- 1/2 teaspoon dried oregano
- 1/2 teaspoon dried basil
- Sea salt, to taste
- 3 ounces edam cheese, shredded
- 1 tablespoon fresh cilantro, chopped
- 1/2 tablespoon fresh tarragon, chopped

## Nutritional Information

308 Calories
24.1g Fat;
6.1g Total Carbs
17.9g Protein
2.8g Fiber

## Directions

Drizzle the melted ghee over your portobellos. Sprinkle the smoked paprika, cayenne pepper, black pepper, oregano, basil, and salt over your mushrooms.

Roast in the preheated oven at 370 degrees F for about 35 minutes or until they have softened; at the halfway point, turn them over to ensure even cooking.

Scatter the edam cheese over your mushrooms and roast an additional 4 to 5 minutes or until it is bubbling.

Serve warm, garnished with fresh cilantro and tarragon. Bon appétit!

# 2. Caprese Asparagus Salad

2 Servings 20 minutes

## Ingredients

- 1 teaspoon fresh lime juice
- 1 tablespoon hot Hungarian paprika in-fused oil
- 1/2 teaspoon kosher salt
- 1/4 teaspoon red pepper flakes
- 1/2 pound asparagus spears, trimmed
- 1 cup grape tomatoes, halved
- 2 tablespoon red wine vinegar
- 1 garlic clove, pressed
- 1-2 drops liquid stevia
- 1 tablespoon fresh basil
- 1 tablespoon fresh chives
- 1/2 cup mozzarella, grated

## Nutritional Information

187 Calories
13.3g Fat
7.4g Total Carbs
9.5g Protein
3.4g Fiber

## Directions

Heat your grill to the hottest setting. Toss your asparagus with the lime juice, hot Hungarian paprika infused oil, salt, and red pepper flakes.

Place the asparagus spears on the hot grill. Grill until one side chars; then, grill your asparagus on the other side.

Cut the asparagus spears into bite-sized pieces and transfer to a salad bowl. Add the grape tomatoes, red wine, garlic, stevia, basil, and chives; toss to combine well.

Top with freshly grated mozzarella cheese and serve immediately.

2 Servings

30 minutes

# 3. Italian-Style Stuffed Peppers

## Ingredients

- 1 tablespoon canola oil
- 1 garlic clove, pressed
- 1/2 cup celery, finely chopped
- 1/2 Spanish onion, finely chopped
- 4 ounces pork, ground
- Sea salt, to taste
- 1 teaspoon Italian seasoning mix
- 2 sweet Italian peppers, deveined and halved
- 1 large-sized Roma tomato, pureed
- 1/2 cup cheddar cheese, grated

## Nutritional Information

313 Calories
21.3g Fat
5.7g Total Carbs
20.2g Protein
1.9g Fiber

## Directions

Heat the canola oil in a sauté pan over medium-high heat. Now, sauté the garlic, celery, and onion until they have softened.

Stir in the ground pork and cook for a further 3 minutes or until no longer pink. Sprinkle with salt and Italian seasoning mix. Divide the filling mixture between the pepper halves.

Add the pureed tomato to a lightly greased baking dish; place the stuffed peppers in the baking dish.

Bake in the preheated oven at 390 degrees F for 20 minutes. Top with the cheddar cheese and bake an additional 4 to 6 minutes or until the cheese is bubbling. Serve warm and enjoy!

# 4. Spicy Glazed Eggplant

2 Servings 20 minutes

## Ingredients

- 1 teaspoon basil
- 1/2 teaspoon oregano
- 1/2 teaspoon rosemary
- 1/2 teaspoon coarse sea salt
- 1 large-sized eggplant, curt into slices lengthwise
- 2 tablespoons coconut aminos
- 1 teaspoon balsamic vinegar
- 1 tablespoon olive oil
- 1/2 teaspoon Sriracha sauce
- 1/4 cup fresh chives, chopped

## Nutritional Information

102 Calories
7g Fat
8g Total Carbs
1.6g Protein
4.7g Fiber

## Directions

Toss your eggplant with the basil, oregano, rosemary, and salt.

Place the eggplant on a parchment-lined roasting pan. Roast in the preheated oven at 420 degrees F approximately 15 minutes.

Meanwhile, mix the coconut aminos, vinegar, oil, and Sriracha sauce. Drizzle the Sriracha mixture over the eggplant slices.

Place under the preheated broil for 3 to 5 minutes. Garnish with fresh chives and serve warm.

# 5. Indian Cabbage Stir-Fry

2 Servings 25 minutes

## Ingredients

- 2 tablespoons olive oil
- 1 (1-inch) piece fresh ginger, grated
- 1/2 teaspoon cumin seeds
- 1 shallot, chopped
- 1/2 cup chicken stock
- 3/4 pound green cabbage, sliced
- 1/4 teaspoon turmeric powder
- 1/2 teaspoon coriander powder
- Kosher salt and cayenne pepper, to taste

## Nutritional Information

168 Calories
13g Fat
7g Total Carbs
2.6g Protein
4.1g Fiber

## Directions

Heat the olive oil in a saucepan over medium heat; then, sauté the ginger and cumin seeds until fragrant.

Add in the shallot and continue sautéing an additional 2 to 3 minutes or until just tender and aromatic. Pour in the chicken stock to deglaze the pan.

Add the cabbage wedges, turmeric, coriander, salt, and cayenne pepper. Cover and cook for 15 to 18 minutes or until your cabbage has softened. Make sure to stir occasionally.

Serve in individual bowls and enjoy!

# 6. Roasted Globe Artichokes with Cheese

2 Servings 10 minutes

## Ingredients

- 2 tablespoons fresh lime juice
- 2 tablespoons butter, melted
- 2 small-sized globe artichokes
- 1/2 teaspoon coriander powder
- 1/4 teaspoon sea salt, or more to taste
- 1/4 teaspoon cayenne pepper, or more to taste
- 1/4 teaspoon hot paprika
- 1 teaspoon capers
- 1/2 teaspoon garlic powder
- 1/2 cup Romano cheese, grated
- 2 tablespoons mayonnaise

## Nutritional Information

368 Calories
33g Fat
7.2g Total Carbs
10.6g Protein
3.8g Fiber

## Directions

To clean your artichokes, cut off the stalks and discard the tough outer layers. Then, cut off about 3/4 inches from the top. Slice your artichokes in half lengthwise.

Toss your artichokes with the fresh lime juice, melted butter, coriander powder, salt, cayenne pepper, paprika, capers, and garlic powder.

Top with the grated Romano cheese. Double wrap your artichokes with 2 layers of heavy-duty foil, sealing well on top.

Roast them at 420 degrees F for 1 hour 5 minutes. When cool enough to handle, unwrap your artichokes and serve with mayonnaise. Bon appétit!

2 Servings 15 minutes

# 7. Spanish Ensalada de Pimientos Rojos

## Ingredients

- 2 red peppers, deveined and sliced
- 1 jarred piquillo pepper, sliced
- 1 garlic clove, minced
- Sea salt and black pepper, to taste
- 1/2 Spanish onion, chopped
- 2 tablespoons wine vinegar
- 2 tablespoons herb infused olive oil
- A pinch of red pepper flakes
- 2 ounces arbequina olives

## Nutritional Information

195 Calories
18.1g Fat
8.1g Total Carbs
1.5g Protein
2.5g Fiber

## Directions

Toss your peppers with the garlic, salt, and black pepper into a stone baking dish.

Bake in the preheated oven at 400 degrees F for 8 to 10 minutes or until your garlic is just starting to toast and the peppers are fragrant and slightly charred.

Transfer to a salad bowl; let it cool to room temperature.

Next, add in the other ingredients; toss to combine well. Enjoy!

# 8. Cheesy Zucchini Fritters

2 Servings 15 minutes

## Ingredients

- 2 tablespoons olive oil
- 3 eggs, whisked
- 1 teaspoon garlic, pressed
- 1/2 pound zucchini, grated
- 1/3 cup almond meal
- 2 tablespoons pork rinds
- 1/4 teaspoon paprika
- Sea salt and ground black pepper, to taste
- 1/2 cup Swiss cheese, shredded

## Nutritional Information

463 Calories
36g Fat
7.6g Total Carbs
27.5g Protein
2.8g Fiber

## Directions

Add the grated zucchini to a colander. Add 1/2 teaspoon of salt, toss and let it sit for 10 minutes. After that, drain the zucchini completely using a cheese cloth.

Heat the olive oil in a skillet over medium-high flame. In a mixing bowl, combine the zucchini with the remaining ingredients until everything is well incorporated.

Make the fritters, flattening them with a spatula; cook for 2 minutes on both sides. Bon appétit!

# POULTRY

# 9. Cheese and Bacon Stuffed Chicken

2 Servings 30 minutes

## Ingredients

- 2 chicken fillets, skinless and boneless
- 1/2 teaspoon oregano
- 1/2 teaspoon tarragon
- 1/2 teaspoon paprika
- 1/4 teaspoon ground black pepper
- Sea salt, to taste
- 2 (1-ounce) slices bacon
- 2 (1-ounce) slices cheddar cheese
- 1 tomato, sliced

## Nutritional Information

401 Calories
23.9g Fat
3.7g Total Carbs
41.2g Protein
1.2g Fiber

## Directions

Sprinkle the chicken fillets with oregano, tarragon, paprika, black pepper, and salt.

Place the bacon slices and cheese on each chicken fillet. Roll up the fillets and secure with toothpicks. Place the stuffed chicken fillets on a lightly greased baking pan. Scatter the sliced tomato around the fillets.

Bake in the preheated oven at 390 degrees F for 15 minutes; turn on the other side and bake an additional 5 to 10 minutes or until the meat is no longer pink.

Discard the toothpicks and serve immediately. Bon appétit!

2 Servings

1 hour 15minutes

# 10. Warming Turkey and Leek Soup

## Ingredients

- 3 cups water
- 1/2 pound turkey thighs
- 1 cup cauliflower, broken into small florets
- 1 large-sized leek, chopped
- 1 small-sized stalk celery, chopped
- 1/2 head garlic, split horizontally
- 1/4 teaspoon turmeric powder
- 1/4 teaspoon Turkish sumac
- 1/4 teaspoon fennel seeds
- 1/2 teaspoon mustard seeds
- 1 bay laurel
- Sea salt and freshly ground black pepper, to season
- 1 teaspoon coconut aminos
- 1 whole egg

## Nutritional Information

216 Calories
8.1g Fat
6.8g Total Carbs
25.2g Protein
2.1g Fiber

## Directions

Add the water and turkey thighs to a pot and bring it to a rolling boil. Cook for about 40 minutes; discard the bones and shred the meat using two forks.

Stir in the cauliflower, leeks, celery, garlic, and spices. Reduce the heat to simmer and let it cook until everything is heated through, about 30 minutes.

Afterwards, add the coconut aminos and egg; whisk until the egg is well incorporated into the soup. Serve hot and enjoy!

# 11. Grilled Turkey Drumsticks

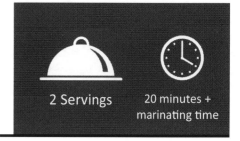

2 Servings

20 minutes + marinating time

## Ingredients

- 1 turkey drumstick, skinless and boneless
- 1 tablespoon balsamic vinegar
- 1 tablespoon whiskey
- 3 tablespoons olive oil
- 1 tablespoon stone ground mustard
- 1/2 teaspoon tarragon
- 1 teaspoon rosemary
- 1 teaspoon sage
- 1 garlic clove, pressed
- Kosher salt and ground black pepper, to season
- 1 brown onion, peeled and chopped

## Directions

Place the turkey drumsticks in a ceramic dish. Toss them with the balsamic vinegar, whiskey, olive oil, mustard, tarragon, rosemary, sage, and garlic.

Cover with plastic wrap and refrigerate for 3 hours. Heat your grill to the hottest setting.

Grill the turkey drumsticks for about 13 minutes per side. Season with salt and pepper to taste and serve with brown onion. Bon appétit!

## Nutritional Information

388 Calories
19.5g Fat
6g Total Carbs
42g Protein
1.4g Fiber

2 Servings

20 minutes + marinating time

# 12. Traditional Turkish Chicken Kebabs

## Ingredients

- 1 pound chicken thighs, boneless, skinless and halved
- 1/2 cup Greek-style yogurt
- Sea salt, to taste
- 1 tablespoon Aleppo red pepper flakes
- 1/2 teaspoon ground black pepper
- 1/4 teaspoon dried oregano
- 1/2 teaspoon mustard seeds
- 1/8 teaspoon ground cinnamon
- 1/2 teaspoon sumac
- 2 Roma tomatoes, chopped
- 2 tablespoons olive oil
- 1 ½ ounces Swiss cheese, sliced

## Nutritional Information

498 Calories
23.2g Fat
6.2g Total Carbs
61g Protein
1.7g Fiber

## Directions

Place the chicken thighs, yogurt, salt, red pepper flakes, black pepper, oregano, mustard seeds, cinnamon, sumac, tomatoes, and olive oil in a ceramic dish. Cover and let it marinate in your refrigerator for 4 hours.

Preheat your grill for medium-high heat and lightly oil the grate. Thread the chicken thighs onto skewers, making a thick log shape.

Cook your kebabs for 3 or 4 minutes; turn over and continue cooking for 3 to 4 minutes more. An instant-read thermometer should read about 165 degrees F.

Add the cheese and let it cook for a further 3 to 4 minutes or until completely melted. Bon appétit!

# 13. Mom's Chicken Salad

2 Servings

20 minutes + chilling time

## Ingredients

- 2 chicken thighs, skinless
- Sea salt and cayenne pepper, to season
- 1/2 teaspoon Dijon mustard
- 1 tablespoon red wine vinegar
- 1/4 cup mayonnaise
- 1 small-sized celery stalk, chopped
- 2 spring onion stalks, chopped
- 1/2 head Romaine lettuce, torn into pieces
- 1/2 cucumber, sliced

## Directions

Fry the chicken thighs until thoroughly heated and crunchy on the outside; an instant-read thermometer should read about 165 degrees F.

Discard the bones and chop the meat.

Place the other ingredients in a serving bowl and stir until everything is well incorporated. Layer the chopped chicken thighs over the salad.

Serve well chilled and enjoy!

## Nutritional Information

456 Calories
29g Fat
6.7g Total Carbs
40.1g Protein
3.7g Fiber

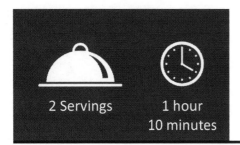

2 Servings

1 hour
10 minutes

# 14. Spring Duck Goulash

## Ingredients

- 2 (1-ounce) slices bacon, chopped
- 1/2 pound duck legs, skinless and boneless
- 2 cups chicken broth, preferably homemade
- 1/2 cup celery ribs, chopped
- 2 green garlic stalks, chopped
- 2 green onion stalks, chopped
- 1 ripe tomato, pureed
- Kosher salt, to season
- 1/4 teaspoon red pepper flakes
- 1/2 teaspoon Hungarian paprika
- 1/2 teaspoon ground black pepper
- 1/2 teaspoon mustard seeds
- 1/2 teaspoon sage
- 1 bay laurel

## Nutritional Information

363 Calories
22.3g Fat
5.1g Total Carbs
33.2g Protein
1.4g Fiber

## Directions

Heat a stockpot over medium-high heat; once hot, fry the bacon until it is crisp or about 3 minutes. Add in the duck legs and cook until they are no longer pink.

Chop the meat, discarding any remaining skin and bones. Then, reserve the bacon and meat.

Pour in a splash of chicken broth to deglaze the pan.

Now, sauté the celery, green garlic and onions for 2 to 3 minutes, stirring periodically. Add the remaining ingredients to the pot, including the reserved bacon and meat.

Stir to combine and reduce the heat to medium-low. Let it cook, covered, until everything is thoroughly heated or about 1 hour. Serve in individual bowls and enjoy!

# 15. Greek-Style Chicken Mélange

2 Servings 35 minutes

## Ingredients

- 2 ounces bacon, diced
- 3/4 pound whole chicken, boneless and chopped
- 1/2 medium-sized leek, chopped
- 1 teaspoon ginger garlic paste
- 1 teaspoon poultry seasoning mix
- Sea salt, to taste
- 1 bay leaf
- 1 thyme sprig
- 1 rosemary sprig
- 1 cup chicken broth
- 1/2 cup cauliflower, chopped into small florets
- 2 vine-ripe tomatoes, pureed

## Nutritional Information

352 Calories
14.3g Fat
5.9g Total Carbs
44.2g Protein
2.4g Fiber

## Directions

Heat a medium-sized pan over medium-high heat; once hot, fry the bacon until it is crisp or about 3 minutes. Add in the chicken and cook until it is no longer pink; reserve.

Then, sauté the leek until tender and fragrant. Stir in the ginger garlic paste, poultry seasoning mix, salt, bay leaf, thyme, and rosemary.

Pour in the chicken broth and reduce the heat to medium; let it cook for 15 minutes, stirring periodically.

Add in the cauliflower and tomatoes along with the reserved bacon and chicken. Decrease the temperature to simmer and let it cook for a further 15 minutes or until warmed through. Bon appétit!

2 Servings 15 minutes

# 16. Teriyaki Turkey Bowls

## Ingredients

- 3/4 pound lean ground turkey
- 1 brown onion, chopped
- 1 red bell pepper, deveined and chopped
- 1 serrano pepper, deveined and chopped
- 1 tablespoon rice vinegar
- 1 garlic clove, pressed
- 1 tablespoon sesame oil
- 1/2 teaspoon ground cumin
- 1/2 teaspoon hot sauce
- 2 tablespoons peanut butter
- Sea salt and cayenne pepper, to season
- 1/2 teaspoon celery seeds
- 1/2 teaspoon mustard seeds
- 1 rosemary sprig, leaves chopped
- 2 tablespoons fresh Thai basil, snipped

## Nutritional Information

410 Calories
27.1g Fat
6.6g Total Carbs
36.5g Protein
1g Fiber

## Directions

Heat a medium-sized pan over medium-high heat; once hot, brown the ground turkey for 4 to 6 minutes; reserve.

Then cook the onion and peppers in the pan drippings for a further 2 to 3 minutes.

Add 1/4 cup of cold water to another saucepan and heat over medium heat. Now, stir in vinegar, garlic, sesame oil, cumin, hot sauce, peanut butter, salt, cayenne pepper, celery seeds, and mustard seeds.

Let it simmer, stirring occasionally, until the mixture begins to bubble slightly. Bring the mixture to a boil; then, immediately remove from the heat and add the cooked ground turkey and sautéed onion/pepper mixture.

Ladle into serving bowls and garnish with the rosemary and Thai basil. Enjoy!

# 17. Sunday Chicken Bake

2 Servings | 30 minutes

## Ingredients

- 1 tablespoon olive oil
- 3/4 pound chicken breast fillets, chopped into bite-sized chunks
- 2 garlic cloves, sliced
- 1/4 teaspoon Korean chili pepper flakes
- 1/4 teaspoon Himalayan salt
- 1/2 teaspoon poultry seasoning mix
- 1 bell pepper, deveined and chopped
- 2 ripe tomatoes, chopped
- 1/4 cup heavy whipping cream
- 1/4 cup sour cream

## Nutritional Information

410 Calories
20.7g Fat
6.2g Total Carbs
50g Protein
1.5g Fiber

## Directions

Brush a casserole dish with olive oil. Add the chicken, garlic, Korean chili pepper flakes, salt, and poultry seasoning mix to the casserole dish.

Next, layer the pepper and tomatoes. Whisk the heavy whipping cream and sour cream in a mixing bowl.

Top everything with the cream mixture. Bake in the preheated oven at 390 degrees F for about 25 minutes or until thoroughly heated. Bon appétit!

# PORK

# 18. Pork Cutlets with Spanish Onion

2 Servings 15 minutes

## Ingredients

- 1 tablespoon olive oil
- 2 pork cutlets
- 1 bell pepper, deveined and sliced
- 1 Spanish onion, chopped
- 2 garlic cloves, minced
- 1/2 teaspoon hot sauce
- 1/2 teaspoon mustard
- 1/2 teaspoon paprika
- Coarse sea salt and ground black pepper, to taste

## Nutritional Information

403 Calories
24.1g Fat
3.4g Total Carbs
40.1g Protein
0.7g Fiber

## Directions

Heat the olive oil in a large saucepan over medium-high heat.

Then, fry the pork cutlets for 3 to 4 minutes until evenly golden and crispy on both sides.

Decrease the temperature to medium and add the bell pepper, Spanish onion, garlic, hot sauce, and mustard; continue cooking until the vegetables have softened, for a further 3 minutes.

Sprinkle with paprika, salt, and black pepper. Serve immediately and enjoy!

2 Servings 40 minutes

# 19. Rich and Easy Pork Ragout

## Ingredients

- 1 teaspoon lard, melted at room temperature
- 3/4 pound pork butt, cut into bite-sized cubes
- 1 red bell pepper, deveined and chopped
- 1 poblano pepper, deveined and chopped
- 2 cloves garlic, pressed
- 1/2 cup leeks, chopped
- Sea salt and ground black pepper, to season
- 1/2 teaspoon mustard seeds
- 1/4 teaspoon ground allspice
- 1/4 teaspoon celery seeds
- 1 cup roasted vegetable broth
- 2 vine-ripe tomatoes, pureed

## Nutritional Information

389 Calories
24.3g Fat
5.4g Total Carbs
33.1g Protein
1.3g Fiber

## Directions

Melt the lard in a stockpot over moderate heat. Once hot, cook the pork cubes for 4 to 6 minutes, stirring occasionally to ensure even cooking.

Then, stir in the vegetables and continue cooking until they are tender and fragrant. Add in the salt, black pepper, mustard seeds, allspice, celery seeds, roasted vegetable broth, and tomatoes.

Reduce the heat to simmer. Let it simmer for 30 minutes longer or until everything is heated through.

Ladle into individual bowls and serve hot. Bon appétit!

# 20. Melt-in-Your-Mouth Pork Roast

2 Servings

1 hour + marinating time

## Ingredients

- 1 pound pork shoulder
- 4 tablespoons red wine
- 1 teaspoon stone ground mustard
- 1 tablespoon coconut aminos
- 1 tablespoon lemon juice
- 1 tablespoon sesame oil
- 2 sprigs rosemary
- 1 teaspoon sage
- 1 shallot, peeled and chopped
- 1/2 celery stalk, chopped
- 1/2 head garlic, peeled and separated into cloves
- Sea salt and freshly cracked black pepper, to season

## Nutritional Information

497 Calories
35.3g Fat
2.5g Total Carbs
40.2g Protein
0.6g Fiber

## Directions

Place the pork shoulder, red wine, mustard, coconut aminos, lemon juice, sesame oil, rosemary, and sage in a ceramic dish; cover and let it marinate in your refrigerator at least 3 hours.

Discard the marinade and place the pork shoulder in a lightly greased baking dish. Scatter the vegetables around the pork shoulder and sprinkle with salt and black pepper.

Roast in the preheated oven at 390 degrees F for 15 minutes.

Now, reduce the temperature to 310 degrees F and continue baking an additional 40 to 45 minutes. Baste the meat with the reserved marinade once or twice.

Place on cooling racks before carving and serving. Bon appétit!

2 Servings 25 minutes

# 21. Chunky Pork Soup with Mustard Greens

## Ingredients

- 1 tablespoon olive oil
- 1 bell pepper, deveined and chopped
- 2 garlic cloves, pressed
- 1/2 cup scallions, chopped
- 1/2 pound ground pork (84% lean)
- 1 cup beef bone broth
- 1 cup water
- 1/2 teaspoon crushed red pepper flakes
- Sea salt and freshly cracked black pepper, to season
- 1 bay laurel
- 1 teaspoon fish sauce
- 2 cups mustard greens, torn into pieces
- 1 tablespoon fresh parsley, chopped

## Nutritional Information

344 Calories
25.2g Fat
6.3g Total Carbs
23.1g Protein
2.9g Fiber

## Directions

Heat the olive oil in a stockpot over a moderate flame. Coat, once hot, sauté the pepper, garlic, and scallions until tender or about 3 minutes.

After that, stir in the ground pork and cook for 5 minutes more or until well browned, stirring periodically.

Add in the beef bone broth, water, red pepper, salt, black pepper, and bay laurel. Reduce the temperature to simmer and cook, covered, for 10 minutes. Afterwards, stir in the fish sauce and mustard greens.

Remove from the heat; let it stand until the greens are wilted. Ladle into individual bowls and serve garnished with fresh parsley.

# 22. Pulled Pork with Mint and Cheese

2 Servings

20 minutes

## Ingredients

- 1 teaspoon lard, melted at room temperature
- 3/4 pork Boston butt, sliced
- 2 garlic cloves, pressed
- 1/2 teaspoon red pepper flakes, crushed
- 1/2 teaspoon black peppercorns, freshly cracked
- Sea salt, to taste
- 2 bell peppers, deveined and sliced
- 1 tablespoon fresh mint leaves, snipped
- 4 tablespoons cream cheese

## Nutritional Information

370 Calories
21.9g Fat
5.1g Total Carbs
34.9g Protein
1g Fiber

## Directions

Melt the lard in a cast-iron skillet over a moderate flame. Once hot, brown the pork for 2 minutes per side until caramelized and crispy on the edges.

Reduce the temperature to medium-low and continue cooking another 4 minutes, turning over periodically. Shred the pork with two forks and return to the skillet.

Add the garlic, red pepper, black peppercorns, salt, and bell pepper and continue cooking for a further 2 minutes or until the peppers are just tender and fragrant.

Serve with fresh mint and a dollop of cream cheese. Enjoy!

2 Servings 15 minutes

# 23. Pork Loin Steaks in Creamy Pepper Sauce

## Ingredients

- 1 teaspoon lard, at room temperature
- 2 pork loin steaks
- 1/2 cup beef bone broth
- 2 bell peppers, deseeded and chopped
- 1 shallot, chopped
- 1 garlic clove, minced
- Sea salt, to season
- 1/2 teaspoon cayenne pepper
- 1/4 teaspoon paprika
- 1 teaspoon Italian seasoning mix
- 1/4 cup Greek-style yogurt

## Nutritional Information

447 Calories
19.2g Fat
6g Total Carbs
62.2g Protein
1.3g Fiber

## Directions

Melt the lard in a cast-iron skillet over moderate heat. Once hot, cook the pork loin steaks until slightly browned or approximately 5 minutes per side; reserve.

Add a splash of the beef bone broth to deglaze the pan. Now, cook the bell peppers, shallot, and garlic until tender and aromatic. Season with salt, cayenne pepper, paprika, and Italian seasoning mix.

After that, decrease the temperature to medium-low, add the Greek yogurt to the skillet and let it simmer for 2 minutes more or until heated through. Serve immediately.

# 24. Pork Medallions with Cabbage

2 Servings  20 minutes

## Ingredients

- 1 ounce bacon, diced
- 2 pork medallions
- 2 garlic cloves, sliced
- 1 red onion, chopped
- 1 jalapeno pepper, deseeded and chopped
- 1 tablespoon apple cider vinegar
- 1/2 cup chicken bone broth
- 1/3 pound red cabbage, shredded
- 1 bay leaf
- 1 sprig rosemary
- 1 sprig thyme
- Kosher salt and ground black pepper, to taste

## Nutritional Information

528 Calories
31.8g Fat
6.3g Total Carbs
51.2g Protein
2.6g Fiber

## Directions

Heat a Dutch pot over medium-high heat. Once hot, cook the bacon until it is crisp or about 3 minutes; reserve.

Now, cook the pork medallions in the bacon grease until they are browned on both sides.

Add the remaining ingredients and reduce the heat to medium-low. Let it cook for 13 minutes more, gently stirring periodically to ensure even cooking.

Taste and adjust the seasonings. Serve in individual bowls topped with the reserved fried bacon. Bon appétit!

2 Servings 25 minutes

# 25. Easy Spicy Meatballs

## Ingredients

- 1 tablespoon ground flax seeds
- 2 ounces bacon rinds
- 1/2 pound ground pork
- 1 garlic clove, minced
- 1/2 cup scallions, chopped
- Sea salt and cayenne pepper, to taste
- 1/2 teaspoon smoked paprika
- 1/4 teaspoon ground cumin
- 1/4 teaspoon mustard seeds
- 1/2 teaspoon fennel seeds
- 1/2 teaspoon chili pepper flakes
- 2 tablespoons olive oil

## Nutritional Information

557 Calories
50.1g Fat
2.3g Total Carbs
0.5g Protein
0.9g Fiber

## Directions

In a mixing bowl, thoroughly combine all ingredients, except for the olive oil, until well combined. Form the mixture into balls and set aside.

Heat the olive oil in a nonstick skillet and fry the meatballs for about 15 minutes or until cooked through.

Serve with marinara sauce if desired. Bon appétit!

# BEEF

2 Servings

1 hour

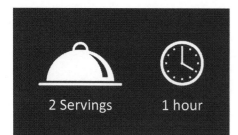

# 26. Mom's Festive Meatloaf

## Ingredients

- 1/4 pound ground pork
- 1/2 pound ground chuck
- 2 eggs, beaten
- 1/4 cup flaxseed meal
- 1 shallot, chopped
- 2 garlic cloves, minced
- 1/4 teaspoon ground black pepper, or more to taste
- 1/2 teaspoon smoked paprika
- 1/4 teaspoon dried basil
- 1/4 teaspoon ground cumin
- Kosher salt, to taste
- 1/2 cup tomato puree
- 1 teaspoon mustard
- 1 teaspoon liquid monk fruit

## Nutritional Information

517 Calories
32.3g Fat
8.4g Total Carbs
48.5g Protein
6.5g Fiber

## Directions

In a mixing bowl, thoroughly combine the ground meat, eggs, flaxseed meal, shallot, garlic, and spices.

In another bowl, mix the tomato puree with the mustard and liquid monk fruit; whisk to combine well.

Press the mixture into the loaf pan. Bake in the preheated oven at 360 degrees F for 30 minutes.

Spread the tomato mixture on top of the meatloaf. Return to the oven and bake for 20 to 25 minutes more or until cooked through.

Let it rest for 8 to 10 minutes before slicing. Cut with a serrated bread knife and enjoy!

# 27. Rich Winter Beef Stew

2 Servings 45 minutes

## Ingredients

- 1 ounce bacon, diced
- 3/4 pound well-marbled beef chuck, boneless and cut into 1-1/2-inch pieces
- 1 red bell pepper, chopped
- 1 green bell pepper, chopped
- 2 garlic cloves, minced
- 1/2 cup leeks, chopped
- 1 parsnip, chopped
- Sea salt, to taste
- 1/4 teaspoon mixed peppercorns, freshly cracked
- 2 cups chicken bone broth
- 1 tomato, pureed
- 2 cups kale, torn into pieces
- 1 tablespoon fresh cilantro, roughly chopped

## Nutritional Information

359 Calories
17.8g Fat
5.4g Total Carbs
43g Protein
1g Fiber

## Directions

Heat a Dutch pot over medium-high flame. Now, cook the bacon until it is well browned and crisp; reserve.

Then, cook the beef pieces for 3 to 5 minutes or until just browned on all sides; reserve. After that, sauté the peppers, garlic, leeks, and parsnip in the pan drippings until they are just tender and aromatic.

Add the salt, peppercorns, chicken bone broth, tomato, and reserved beef to the pot. Bring to a boil.

Turn the heat to simmer and let it cook for 25 to 35 minutes more or until everything is cooked through.

Lastly, stir in the kale leaves and continue simmering until the leaves have wilted or 3 to 4 minutes more.

Ladle into individual bowls and serve garnished with fresh cilantro and the reserved bacon. Bon appétit!

2 Servings 35 minutes

# 28. Mini Meatloaves with Spinach

## Ingredients

- 1/2 pound lean ground beef
- 2 tablespoons tomato paste
- 1 teaspoon Dijon mustard
- 1 egg, beaten
- 1/2 teaspoon ginger garlic paste
- 1/2 cup shallots, finely chopped
- 1 tablespoon canola oil
- 1/2 teaspoon coconut aminos
- 1/4 cup almond meal
- 1 bunch spinach, chopped
- 1 teaspoon dried parsley flakes
- 1/2 teaspoon dried basil
- 1/2 teaspoon dried rosemary
- 1/2 teaspoon dried sage
- 1/4 teaspoon cayenne pepper
- Kosher salt and ground black pepper
- 2 tablespoons sour cream

## Nutritional Information

434 Calories
29.4g Fat
4.4g Total Carbs
37.1g Protein
2.1g Fiber

## Directions

Mix all of the above ingredients, except for the sour cream, until everything is well incorporated.

Press the meat mixture into a lightly greased muffin tin. Bake the mini meatloaves in the preheated oven at 360 degrees F for 20 to 28 minutes.

Serve with sour cream and enjoy!

# 29. Beef and Garden Vegetable Soup

2 Servings 35 minutes

## Ingredients

- 1 teaspoon olive oil
- 1/2 pound lean ground beef
- 1/2 cup celery stalks, chopped
- 1/2 cup scallions, chopped
- 1 jalapeno pepper, chopped
- 1 cup green cabbage, shredded
- 2 cups chicken bone broth
- 1/4 teaspoon cayenne pepper
- 1 teaspoon ground coriander
- 1/2 teaspoon ground bay leaf
- Kosher salt and freshly cracked black pepper, to taste
- 1 vine-ripe tomato, pureed
- 1 tablespoon apple cider vinegar

## Directions

Heat the olive oil in a medium-sized stockpot over medium-high flame. Now, brown the ground beef until no longer pink.

Stir in the celery, scallions, and jalapeno pepper

continue cooking an additional 3 minutes or until your vegetables have softened.

Then, stir in the remaining ingredients, cover, and decrease the temperature to medium-low. Let it simmer for 30 minutes or until thoroughly heated. Bon appétit!

## Nutritional Information

299 Calories
15.1g Fat
6.5g Total Carbs
32g Protein
2.7g Fiber

2 Servings

1 hour
10 minutes

# 30. Sunday Roast Beef with Herbs

## Ingredients

- 1 pound rump roast, boneless
- 1 tablespoon yellow mustard
- 1 teaspoon dried thyme
- 1/2 teaspoon dried rosemary
- 1 teaspoon dried parsley flakes
- Sea salt and freshly ground black pepper, to taste
- 1/2 cup beef bone broth
- 4 garlic cloves, peeled and halved
- 2 yellow onions, quartered

## Nutritional Information

316 Calories
13.2g Fat
2.6g Total Carbs
47.2g Protein
0.5g Fiber

## Directions

Pat the roast dry with paper towels. Then, rub the roast with the mustard and spices on all sides. Place the rump roast in a roasting pan; pour in the beef broth.

Scatter the garlic and onions around the meat and transfer to the preheated oven.

Roast at 360 degrees F for 30 minutes. Then lower the heat to 220 degrees F and roast for 30 to 40 minutes more. Bon appétit!

# 31. Mexican-Style Beef Casserole

2 Servings 55 minutes

## Ingredients

- 1 tablespoon canola oil
- 1/2 pound blade steak, sliced into strips
- 1 bell pepper, seeded and chopped
- 1 jalapeno pepper, seeded and chopped
- 1 cup cauliflower florets
- 1 medium-sized leek, thinly sliced
- 1/2 teaspoon Mexican oregano
- 1 teaspoon paprika
- 1 vine-ripe tomato, pureed
- 2 tablespoons apple cider vinegar
- 1/2 cup roasted vegetable broth
- 3/4 cup Manchego cheese, shredded

## Nutritional Information

452 Calories
32.1g Fat
7.1g Total Carbs
39.2g Protein
2.1g Fiber

## Directions

Heat the canola oil in a Dutch oven over medium-high flame. Now, cook the beef for 5 to 6 minutes, stirring periodically to ensure even cooking.

Now, stir in the peppers, cauliflower, and leeks; continue cooking an additional 4 minutes or until the vegetables are tender and aromatic.

Add in the Mexican oregano, paprika, tomatoes, vinegar and broth. Decrease the temperature to simmer and let it cook for a further 30 minutes.

Spoon the mixture into a casserole dish; top with the Manchego and bake for 10 to 13 minutes or until the cheese has melted and the edges are bubbling. Let it rest for 10 minutes before cutting and serving. Enjoy!

2 Servings

1 hour
45 minutes

# 32. Sticky Barbecued Ribs

## Ingredients

- 1 tablespoon olive oil
- 1/2 pound beef ribs
- 1 leek, sliced
- 1/4 cup red wine
- 1/2 cup vegetable broth
- 1/2 teaspoon cumin powder
- 1/2 teaspoon ginger powder
- Kosher salt and cayenne pepper, to taste
- 1 teaspoon liquid smoke
- 1 teaspoon granulated garlic
- 1/4 teaspoon stevia powder
- 1 teaspoon American-style mustard
- 1 tablespoon sesame seeds, toasted
- 2 tablespoons fresh chives, chopped

## Nutritional Information

481 Calories
41g Fat
5.9g Total Carbs
19.9g Protein
1.3g Fiber

## Directions

Heat the olive oil in a pan over a moderate flame. Now, sear the beef ribs for 3 to 4 minutes on each side; stir in the leek and cook an additional 3 minutes.

Add a splash of wine to deglaze the pan. Now, add in the remaining wine, broth, cumin powder, ginger powder, salt, and pepper.

Decrease the temperature to medium-low, cover, and let it cook for 40 minutes. Now, line a baking dish with foil. Place the ribs along with the cooking liquid in the baking dish.

Add in the liquid smoke, garlic, stevia, and American-style mustard. Bake in the preheated oven at 300 degrees F for 1 hour; make sure to turn the ribs periodically to ensure they are coated with the glaze.

Top with sesame seeds and chives. Bon appétit!

# 33. Beef Teriyaki Skillet

2 Servings 15 minutes

## Ingredients

- 1 teaspoon sesame oil
- 3/4 pound flank steak, thinly sliced
- 1 yellow onion, thinly sliced
- 1/2 cup Chinese cabbage, shredded
- 1/2 cup cream of celery soup
- 1/2 teaspoon ginger garlic paste
- 1/2 teaspoon chili flakes
- 1 tablespoon soy sauce
- 1 tablespoon xylitol
- Kosher salt and freshly ground black pepper, to taste

## Nutritional Information

304 Calories
13.7g Fat
5.2g Total Carbs
37.2g Protein
0.8g Fiber

## Directions

Heat the sesame oil in a skillet over moderate heat; sear the meat along with the onion for about 6 minutes or until the meat is no longer pink.

Add the Chinese cabbage and stir for 2 to 3 minutes more; reserve the meat/vegetable mixture.

Stir the remaining ingredients into the skillet and bring to a simmer. Let it cook for 4 to 6 minutes or until heated through and thickened.

Add the sautéed mixture to the skillet and gently stir until everything is well coated with the sauce.

Serve in lettuce wraps if desired. Enjoy!

# FISH & SEAFOOD

# 34. Sea Bass with Vegetables and Dill Sauce

2 Servings
25 minutes

## Ingredients

- 1 tablespoon olive oil
- 1 cup red onions, sliced
- 2 bell peppers, deveined and sliced
- Se salt and cayenne pepper, to taste
- 1 teaspoon paprika
- 1 pound sea bass fillets

**Dill Sauce:**

- 1 tablespoon mayonnaise
- 1/4 cup Greek yogurt
- 1 tablespoon fresh dill, chopped
- 1/2 teaspoon garlic powder
- 1/2 fresh lemon, juiced

## Nutritional Information

374 Calories
17g Fat
6.2g Total Carbs
43.2g Protein
2.2g Fiber

## Directions

Toss the onions, peppers, and sea bass fillets with the olive oil, salt, cayenne pepper, and paprika.

Line a baking pan with a piece of parchment paper. Preheat your oven to 400 degrees F.

Arrange your fish and vegetables on the prepared baking pan. Bake for 10 minutes; turn them over and bake for a further 10 to 12 minutes.

Meanwhile, make the sauce by mixing all ingredients until well combined.

Serve the fish and vegetables with the dill sauce on the side. Bon appétit!

2 Servings 20 minutes

# 35. Roasted Old Bay Prawns

## Ingredients

- 3/4 pound prawns, peeled and deveined
- 1 teaspoon Old Bay seasoning mix
- 1/2 teaspoon paprika
- Coarse sea salt and ground black pepper, to taste
- 1 habanero pepper, deveined and minced
- 1 bell pepper, deveined and minced
- 1 cup pound broccoli florets
- 2 teaspoons olive oil
- 1 tablespoon fresh chives, chopped
- 2 slices lemon, for garnish
- 2 dollops of sour cream, for garnish

## Nutritional Information

269 Calories
9.6g Fat
7.2g Total Carbs
38.2g Protein
2.5g Fiber

## Directions

Toss the prawns with the Old Bay seasoning mix, paprika, salt, and black pepper.

Arrange them on a parchment-lined roasting pan. Add the bell pepper and broccoli. Drizzle olive oil over everything and transfer the pan to a preheated oven.

Roast at 390 degrees F for 8 to 11 minutes, turning the pan halfway through the cooking time. Bake until the prawns are pink and cooked through.

Serve with fresh chives, lemon, and sour cream. Bon appétit!

# 36. Hungarian Fish Paprikash (Halászlé)

2 Servings 20 minutes

## Ingredients

- 1 tablespoon canola oil
- 2 bell peppers, chopped
- 1 Hungarian wax pepper, chopped
- 1 garlic clove, minced
- 1 red onion, chopped
- 1/2 pound tilapia, cut into bite-sized pieces
- 1 ½ cups fish broth
- 2 vine-ripe tomatoes, pureed
- 1 teaspoon sweet paprika
- 1/2 teaspoon mixed peppercorns, crushed
- 1 bay laurel
- 1/2 teaspoon sumac
- 1/2 teaspoon dried thyme
- 1/4 teaspoon dried rosemary
- Kosher salt, to season
- 1/2 teaspoon garlic, minced
- 2 tablespoons sour cream

## Nutritional Information

252 Calories
12.6g Fat
5g Total Carbs
28.2g Protein
1.9g Fiber

## Directions

Heat the canola oil in a Dutch oven over medium-high heat. Now, sauté the peppers, garlic, and onion until tender and aromatic.

Now, stir in the tilapia, broth, tomatoes, and spices. Reduce the heat to medium-low. Let it simmer, covered, for 9 to 13 minutes.

Meanwhile, mix 1/2 teaspoon of minced garlic with the sour cream. Serve with the warm paprikash and enjoy!

2 Servings

20 minutes

# 37. Easy Baked Halibut Steaks

## Ingredients

- 2 tablespoons olive oil
- 2 halibut steaks
- 1 red bell pepper, sliced
- 1 yellow onion, sliced
- 1 teaspoon garlic, smashed
- 1/2 teaspoon hot paprika
- Sea salt cracked black pepper, to your liking
- 1 dried thyme sprig, leaves crushed

## Nutritional Information

502 Calories
19.1g Fat
5.7g Total Carbs
72g Protein
1g Fiber

## Directions

Start by preheating your oven to 390 degrees F.

Then, drizzle olive oil over the halibut steaks. Place the halibut in a baking dish that is previously greased with a nonstick spray.

Top with the bell pepper, onion, and garlic. Sprinkle hot paprika, salt, black pepper, and dried thyme over everything.

Bake in the preheated oven for 13 to 15 minutes and serve immediately. Enjoy!

# 38. Easiest Fish Jambalaya Ever

2 Servings 15 minutes

## Ingredients

- 1 teaspoon canola oil
- 1 jalapeno pepper, minced
- 1 small-sized leek, chopped
- 1/2 teaspoon ginger garlic paste
- 1/4 teaspoon ground cumin
- 1/4 teaspoon ground allspice
- 1/2 teaspoon oregano
- 1/4 teaspoon thyme
- 1/4 teaspoon marjoram
- 1 pound sole fish fillets, cut into bite-sized strips
- 1 large-sized ripe tomato, pureed
- 1/2 cup water
- 1/2 cup clam juice
- Kosher salt, to season
- 1 bay laurel
- 5-6 black peppercorns
- 1 cup spinach, torn into pieces

## Nutritional Information

232 Calories
3.6g Fat
6.7g Total Carbs
38.1g Protein
2.1g Fiber

## Directions

Heat the oil in a Dutch oven over a moderate flame. Then, sauté the pepper and leek until they have softened.

Now, stir in the ginger-garlic paste, cumin, allspice, oregano, thyme, and marjoram; continue stirring for 30 to 40 seconds more or until aromatic.

Add in the fish, tomatoes, water, clam juice, salt, bay laurel, and black peppercorns. Cover and decrease the temperature to medium-low.

Let it simmer for 4 to 6 minutes or until the liquid has reduced slightly. Stir in the spinach and let it simmer, covered, for about 2 minutes more or until it wilts.

Ladle into serving bowls and serve warm. Bon appétit!

2 Servings 20 minutes

# 39. Saucy Cod with Mustard Greens

## Ingredients

- 1 tablespoon olive oil
- 1 bell pepper, seeded and sliced
- 1 jalapeno pepper, seeded and sliced
- 2 stalks green onions, sliced
- 1 stalk green garlic, sliced
- 1/2 cup fish broth
- 2 cod fish fillets
- 1/2 teaspoon paprika
- Sea salt and ground black pepper, to season
- 1 cup mustard greens, torn into bite-sized pieces

## Directions

Heat the olive oil in a Dutch pot over a moderate flame. Now, sauté the peppers, green onions, and garlic until just tender and aromatic.

Add in the broth, fish fillets, paprika, salt, black pepper, and mustard greens. Reduce the temperature to medium-low, cover, and let it cook for 11 to 13 minutes or until heated through.

Serve immediately garnished with lemon slices if desired. Bon appétit!

## Nutritional Information

171 Calories
7.8g Fat
4.8g Total Carbs
20.3g Protein
1.6g Fiber

# 40. Skillet Shrimp and Sea Scallop with Scallions

2 Servings 15 minutes

## Ingredients

- 1 tablespoon olive oil
- 1/2 cup scallions, chopped
- 1 garlic clove, minced
- 1/2 pound shrimp, deveined
- 1/2 pound sea scallops
- 2 tablespoons rum
- 1/2 cup fish broth
- 1/4 teaspoon Cajun seasoning mix
- Sea salt and ground black pepper, to taste
- 1 tablespoon fresh parsley, chopped

## Nutritional Information

305 Calories
8.8g Fat
2.7g Total Carbs
47.3g Protein
0.7g Fiber

## Directions

In a sauté pan, heat the olive oil until sizzling. Now, sauté your scallions and garlic until they are just tender and fragrant.

Now, sear the shrimp and sea scallops for 2 to 3 minutes or until they are firm. Add a splash of rum to deglaze the pan. Now, pour in the fish broth.

Add in the Cajun seasoning mix, salt, and black pepper; stir and remove from heat.

Serve warm garnished with fresh parsley. Enjoy!

2 Servings 15 minutes

# 41. Asian-Style Fish Salad

## Ingredients

**Salad:**

- 1/4 cup water
- 1/4 cup Sauvignon Blanc
- 1/2 pound salmon fillets
- 1 cup Chinese cabbage, sliced
- 1 tomato, sliced
- 2 radishes, sliced
- 1 bell pepper, sliced
- 1 medium-sized white onion, sliced

**Salad Dressing:**

- 1/2 teaspoon fresh garlic, minced
- 1 fresh chili pepper, seeded and minced
- 1/2 teaspoon fresh ginger, peeled and grated
- 2 tablespoons fresh lime juice
- 1 tablespoon sesame oil
- 1 tablespoon tamari sauce
- 1 teaspoon xylitol
- 1 tablespoon fresh mint, roughly chopped
- Sea salt and freshly ground black pepper, to taste

## Directions

Place the water and Sauvignon Blanc in a sauté pan; bring to a simmer over moderate heat.

Place the salmon fillets, skin-side down in the pan and cover with the lid. Cook for 5 to 8 minutes or to your desired doneness; do not overcook the salmon; reserve.

Place the Chinese cabbage, tomato, radishes, bell pepper, and onion in a serving bowl.

Prepare the salad dressing by whisking all ingredients. Dress your salad, top with the salmon fillets and serve immediately!

## Nutritional Information

277 Calories
15.1g Fat
4.9g Total Carbs
24.4g Protein
0.9g Fiber

# EGGS & DAIRY

2 Servings 15 minutes

# 42. Omelet with Vegetables and Mexican Cotija Cheese

## Ingredients

- 2 teaspoons olive oil
- 2 scallion stalks, chopped
- 2 garlic cloves, minced
- 2 bell peppers, chopped
- 1/2 cup cauliflower florets
- 3 eggs
- 1/2 teaspoon cayenne pepper
- Kosher salt and ground black pepper, to season
- 1/2 teaspoon dried Mexican oregano
- 1/2 teaspoon chili pepper flakes
- 1/2 teaspoon dried parsley flakes
- 2 ounces Cotija cheese, crumbled

## Nutritional Information

287 Calories
20.5g Fat
7.2g Total Carbs
17.4g Protein
2.9g Fiber

## Directions

Heat the olive oil in a medium-sized pan over moderate heat. Sauté the scallions and garlic until just tender and fragrant.

Now, stir in the peppers and cauliflower and continue sautéing an additional 2 to 3 minutes.

Meanwhile, mix the eggs with the cayenne pepper, salt, black pepper, oregano, chili pepper flakes, and parsley.

Pour the egg mixture over the sautéed vegetables. Let it cook, tilting your pan so the raw parts can cook.

Add the Cotija cheese, fold over and leave for 1 minute before slicing and serving. Enjoy!

# 43. Spicy Masala and Brown Mushroom Omelet

2 Servings 15 minutes

## Ingredients

- 1 tablespoon olive oil
- 1/2 brown onion, thinly sliced
- 1 garlic clove, thinly sliced
- 1 green chili, minced
- 1/2 pound brown mushrooms, sliced
- 4 eggs, whisked
- 1 tablespoon fresh coriander, chopped
- Sea salt and ground black pepper, to taste
- 1/2 tsp Kashmiri chili powder
- 1/2 teaspoon garam masala

## Nutritional Information

217 Calories
15.6g Fat
5g Total Carbs
14.4g Protein
1.2g Fiber

## Directions

In a nonstick skillet, heat the olive oil until sizzling. Then, sauté the onion until translucent. Now, stir in the garlic, chili pepper, and mushrooms and continue sautéing until just tender and fragrant or about 2 minutes. Reserve.

Add in the whisked eggs, fresh coriander, salt, black pepper, Kashmiri chili powder, and garam masala. Give it a quick swirl to distribute the eggs evenly across the skillet. Cook for 2 to 3 minutes.

Flip your omelet over and cook an additional minute or so. Fill with the mushroom mixture, fold and serve immediately. Bon appétit!

2 Servings 15 minutes

# 44. Classic Egg Salad

## Ingredients

- 3 eggs
- 1/4 cup scallions, chopped
- 1 jalapeno pepper, deseeded and minced
- 1/4 cup mayonnaise
- 1 teaspoon Dijon mustard
- Kosher salt and ground black pepper, to taste
- 1 tablespoon fresh parsley, roughly chopped
- 1/2 teaspoon sweet paprika

## Nutritional Information

398 Calories
35.2g Fat
5.5g Total Carbs
14.6g Protein
1g Fiber

## Directions

Arrange the eggs in a small saucepan. Pour in water (1-inch above the eggs) and bring to a boil.

Heat off and let it sit, covered, for 9 to 10 minutes.

When the eggs are cool enough to handle, peel away the shells, and rinse the eggs under running water. Chop the eggs and transfer them to a serving bowl.

Add in the scallions, jalapeno pepper, mayonnaise, mustard, salt, and black pepper.

Sprinkle fresh parsley and paprika over the salad and serve well chilled.

# 45. Swiss Cheese Soup

2 Servings 15 minutes

## Ingredients

- 2 tablespoons ghee, at room temperature
- 1/2 cup shallots, chopped
- 1/2 cup cream of onion soup
- 1/2 cup water
- 1 cup yogurt
- 4 ounces Swiss cheese, shredded

## Nutritional Information

365 Calories
27.2g Fat
6.6g Total Carbs
21g Protein
0.8g Fiber

## Directions

Melt the ghee in a pot over a moderate flame; now, sauté the shallots until just tender and fragrant or about 3 minutes.

Stir in the cream of onion soup and water. Turn the heat to simmer and let it cook for 10 minutes more or until everything is heated through.

Heat off; fold in the yogurt and cheese. Whisk until everything is well incorporated and the cheese completely melts.

Ladle into individual bowls. Bon appétit!

2 Servings 10 minutes

# 46. Italian-Style Keto Sandwiches

## Ingredients

- 1 tablespoon butter
- 2 eggs
- 4 thin zucchini slices, cut lengthwise
- 2 slices provolone cheese
- 2 slices Genoa salami
- 2 slices Sopressata
- 1 red bell pepper, sliced thinly
- 1/2 teaspoon chipotle in adobo sauce, minced
- 1 clove garlic, minced
- 2 basil leaves, snipped
- Sea salt and ground black pepper, to taste

## Directions

Melt the butter in a nonstick skillet over medium-high heat. Now, crack the eggs and cook until they are set, about 4 to 5 minutes.

Place one zucchini slice on two plates. Add the cheese, Genoa salami, Sopressata, peppers, and garlic to each of the zucchini slices.

Top with the fried eggs

sprinkle with basil, salt, and pepper and top with the remaining zucchini slices. Enjoy!

## Nutritional Information

352 Calories
26.5g Fat
6.6g Total Carbs
22.1g Protein
0.6g Fiber

# 47. Homemade Fluffy Tortillas with Cheese

2 Servings 10 minutes

## Ingredients

- 1 tablespoon almond meal
- 1 tablespoon flax seed meal
- 1 tablespoon ground sunflower seed
- 1/4 teaspoon baking powder
- 2 tablespoons full-fat milk
- 2 eggs
- 3 ounces cheddar cheese, sliced

## Nutritional Information

393 Calories
31.7g Fat
5.1g Total Carbs
22.8g Protein
1.6g Fiber

## Directions

In a mixing dish, thoroughly combine the almond meal, flax seed meal, ground sunflower seed, and baking powder; mix to combine well.

In another dish, whisk the milk and eggs until frothy; add the egg mixture to the dry flour mixture. Mix to combine well.

Heat up a lightly greased skillet over a medium-high flame. Fry your tortillas for 2 minutes. Flip it over and continue cooking for a minute or so until lightly golden on both sides.

Add the cheddar cheese, roll them up, and serve or keep them warm until serving. Bon appétit!

2 Servings 15 minutes

# 48. Frittata with Kale and Cheese

## Ingredients

- 1 tablespoon olive oil
- 1 white onion, chopped
- 1 teaspoon garlic, minced
- 1 cup kale, torn into pieces
- 4 eggs
- 4 tablespoons sour cream
- Sea salt and ground black pepper, to season
- 1 tablespoon fresh coriander, chopped
- 1/2 teaspoon dried oregano
- 1/2 teaspoon hot paprika
- 1/2 cup Monterey-Jack cheese, shredded

## Nutritional Information

417 Calories
34.5g Fat
5.3g Total Carbs
20.6g Protein
1.1g Fiber

## Directions

Heat the olive oil in an oven-proof pan over medium-high flame. Now, sauté the onion and garlic until they are tender and fragrant or about 3 minutes.

Now, add in the kale leaves and stir for about 40 seconds or until they wilt.

In a mixing bowl, thoroughly combine the eggs with the sour cream, salt, and black pepper. Pour the mixture into the pan and tilt until it is evenly distributed.

Add in the coriander, oregano, and paprika. Top with the shredded cheese.

Bake in the preheated oven at 390 degrees F for 9 to 11 minutes until the eggs are puffed; do not overcook your frittata.

Let it sit for 10 minutes before slicing and serving. Bon appétit!

# 49. Breakfast Keto Muffins

2 Servings 30 minutes

## Ingredients

- 1 teaspoon butter, softened at room temperature
- 2 ounces ham, chopped
- 2 scallion stalks, chopped
- 2 garlic cloves, minced
- 1 bell pepper, diced
- 1 cup broccoli florets
- 2 tablespoons tomato paste
- 1/4 cup double cream
- 4 eggs
- 1/4 cup mozzarella cheese, shredded
- Sea salt and cayenne pepper, to taste

## Nutritional Information

299 Calories
20.2g Fat
6.7g Total Carbs
21.5g Protein
2.2g Fiber

## Directions

Melt the butter in a nonstick skillet over a moderate flame. Now, sauté the ham together with the scallions, garlic, pepper, and broccoli until they are tender and fragrant.

In a mixing bowl, thoroughly combine the tomato paste with the double cream, eggs, mozzarella, salt, and cayenne pepper.

Fold in the sautéed mixture and stir to combine well. Spoon the mixture into muffin pans, filling each cup about two-thirds full.

Bake in the preheated oven at 360 degrees F for 12 to 13 minutes or until a toothpick inserted into a muffin comes out dry and clean.

Transfer them to a cooling rack for 10 minutes before unmolding and serving. Bon appétit!

# VEGETARIAN

# 50. Easy Zoodles with Sauce and Parmesan

2 Servings 10 minutes

## Ingredients

- 1/2 avocado, pitted and peeled
- 2 tablespoons sunflower seeds, hulled
- 1 ripe tomato, quartered
- 2 tablespoons water
- Sea salt and ground black pepper, to taste
- 1/4 teaspoon dried dill weed
- 1 medium-sized zucchini, sliced
- 2 tablespoons parmesan cheese, preferably freshly grated

## Directions

In your blender or food processor, puree the avocado, sunflower seeds, tomato, water, salt, black pepper, and dill until creamy and uniform.

Prepare your zoodles using a spiralizer.

Top the zoodles with the sauce; serve garnished with parmesan cheese. Bon appétit!

## Nutritional Information

164 Calories
13.3g Fat
8.7g Total Carbs
5.5g Protein
4.9g Fiber

2 Servings 20 minutes

# 51. Authentic Thai Tom Kha Soup

## Ingredients

- 1 teaspoon coconut oil
- 1 shallot, chopped
- 1 clove garlic, minced
- 1/2 celery stalk, chopped
- 1/2 bell pepper, chopped
- 1 Bird's eye chili, divined and minced
- 1 cup vegetable broth
- 1/4 teaspoon stone ground mustard
- Sea salt and freshly cracked black pepper, to season
- 1/2 teaspoon ground cumin
- 1/2 teaspoon coriander seeds
- 2 cardamom pods
- 1 cup coconut milk, full-fat
- 2 tablespoons Thai basil leaves, snipped

## Nutritional Information

273 Calories
27.3g Fat
5.7g Total Carbs
5.2g Protein
0.5g Fiber

## Directions

In a deep saucepan, heat the coconut oil until sizzling; now, sauté the shallot, garlic, celery, and peppers until just tender and fragrant; make sure to stir frequently.

Add a splash of broth to deglaze the pan. Add in the remaining broth, mustard, and spices and bring to a rolling boil.

Turn the heat to medium-low and let it simmer for 15 minutes or until heated through. After that, pour in the coconut milk and continue to simmer for 2 minutes more.

Ladle into soup bowls and serve garnished with fresh Thai basil. Enjoy!

# 52. Zucchini and Mushroom Lasagna

2 Servings

1 hour 20 minutes

## Ingredients

- 1 large-sized zucchini, sliced lengthwise
- 1 tablespoon olive oil
- 1 red bell pepper, chopped
- 1 shallot, chopped
- 1/2 pound chestnut mushrooms, chopped
- 2 cloves garlic, pressed
- Sea salt and ground black pepper, to season
- 1/4 teaspoon red pepper flakes
- 1/4 teaspoon dried oregano
- 1/2 teaspoon dried dill weed
- 1 vine-ripe tomato, pureed
- 1 egg, whisked
- 1/2 cup Greek-style yogurt
- 1/2 cup Provolone cheese, grated

## Nutritional Information

284 Calories
18.3g Fat
7.9g Total Carbs
20g Protein
2.9g Fiber

## Directions

Place the zucchini slices in a bowl with a colander; add 1 teaspoon of salt and let it stand for 12 to 15 minutes; gently squeeze to discard the excess water.

Grill the zucchini slices for 3 minutes per side until beginning to brown; reserve.

Heat the olive oil in a skillet over moderate flame. Now, sauté the pepper and shallot until they have softened.

Next, stir in the mushrooms and garlic; continue sautéing until they are just fragrant. Add in the spices and pureed tomatoes and let it cook until heated through or about 5 minutes.

Pour the mushroom/tomato sauce on the bottom of a lightly greased baking pan. Arrange the zucchini slices on top.

Mix the egg with the Greek yogurt; add the mixture to the top. Top with the grated Provolone cheese and transfer to the preheated oven.

Bake at 370 degrees F approximately 45 minutes until the cheese is melted and the edges are bubbling.

Let your lasagna stand for about 8 minutes before slicing and serving. Bon appétit!

2 Servings 35 minutes

# 53. Double Cheese Baked Stuffed Peppers

## Ingredients

- 1 garlic clove, minced
- 2 scallions, chopped
- 3 ounces cream cheese
- 3 eggs
- 3 ounces provolone cheese, grated
- Sea salt and ground black pepper, to taste
- 1/2 teaspoon hot paprika
- 1 teaspoon coriander
- 3 bell peppers, deseeded and sliced in half
- 4 Kalamata olives, pitted and sliced

## Nutritional Information

387 Calories
30.3g Fat
5.3g Total Carbs
22.7g Protein
0.9g Fiber

## Directions

In a mixing bowl, thoroughly combine the garlic, scallions, cream cheese, eggs, provolone cheese, salt, black pepper, paprika, and coriander.

Stuff the peppers and place them on a parchment lined baking sheet.

Bake in the preheated oven at 370 degrees F approximately 30 minutes until the peppers are tender. If you want your peppers nicely charred, just place them under the broiler for 2 minutes.

Garnish with olives and serve immediately. Bon appétit!

# 54. Broccoli Slaw with Tahini Dressing

2 Servings 10 minutes

## Ingredients

**Salad:**

- 1/2 cup broccoli florets
- 1 bell pepper, seeded and sliced
- 1 shallot, thinly sliced
- 1/2 cup arugula
- 2 ounces mozzarella cheese
- 2 tablespoons toasted sunflower seeds

**Tahini Dressing:**

- 1 tablespoon freshly squeezed lemon juice
- 1/4 cup tahini (sesame butter)
- 1 garlic clove, minced
- 1/2 teaspoon yellow mustard
- 1/2 teaspoon ground black pepper
- Pink salt, to taste

## Nutritional Information

323 Calories
25.3g Fat
6.8g Total Carbs
15.7g Protein
3.4g Fiber

## Directions

Place the cabbage, pepper, shallot, and arugula in a nice salad bowl. Mix all ingredients for the dressing.

Now, dress your salad and top with the mozzarella cheese and sunflower seeds.

Serve at room temperature or well chilled. Bon appétit!

2 Servings 15 minutes

# 55. Keto Tabbouleh Salad

## Ingredients

- 1 cup cauliflower florets
- 1 tablespoon fresh mint leaves, roughly chopped
- 1 tablespoon fresh parsley leaves, roughly chopped
- 1/2 white onion, thinly sliced
- 1/2 cup cherry tomatoes, halved
- 1 Lebanese cucumber, diced
- Pink salt and freshly cracked black pepper, to taste
- 1 tablespoon hulled hemp seeds
- 1 tablespoon fresh lemon juice
- 2 tablespoons extra-virgin olive oil

## Nutritional Information

180 Calories
16.1g Fat
7g Total Carbs
2.7g Protein
2.7g Fiber

## Directions

Pulse the cauliflower florets in your food processor until they're broken into tiny chunks (just bigger than rice).

Pat dry with paper towels. Cook in a lightly greased nonstick skillet over medium heat until the cauliflower rice is turning golden or about 8 minutes; transfer to a serving bowl.

Add the remaining ingredients and toss to combine well.

Adjust the seasonings and serve. Enjoy!

# 56. Easy Creamy Broccoli Soup

2 Servings 15 minutes

## Ingredients

- 1 tablespoon butter, at room temperature
- 1/2 small-sized leek, chopped
- 1/4 cup celery rib, chopped
- 1/2 teaspoon ginger garlic paste
- 1 ½ cups broccoli florets
- 1 ½ cups roasted vegetable broth
- 1 bay laurel
- 1 thyme sprig, chopped
- 1 cup spinach leaves
- Kosher salt and ground black pepper, to taste
- 2 tablespoons cream cheese
- 1 tablespoon tahini butter
- 1/3 cup yogurt

## Nutritional Information

208 Calories
15.9g Fat
6.4g Total Carbs
8.8g Protein
3g Fiber

## Directions

In a Dutch pot, melt the butter over medium-high heat. Now, sauté the leeks and celery until just tender and fragrant.

Add the ginger-garlic paste and continue cooking an additional 30 seconds or until aromatic.

Now, stir in the broccoli, broth, bay laurel, and thyme, and bring it to a rapid boil. Then, turn the heat to low and let it simmer, covered, for a further 5 to 8 minutes.

After that, stir in the spinach, salt, and black pepper; let it simmer for 2 minutes more or until the leaves have wilted.

Transfer the soup to a food processor; add the cream cheese and tahini butter; process until everything is smooth and uniform. Swirl the yogurt into the soup and serve warm. Bon appétit!

2 Servings 1 hour

# 57. Mediterranean Cauliflower Quiche with Cheese

## Ingredients

- 1/2 pound small cauliflower florets
- 1/2 cup vegetable broth
- 2 scallions, chopped
- 1 teaspoon garlic, crushed
- 1/2 cup full-fat milk
- 2 eggs, whisked
- Sea salt and ground black pepper, to taste
- 1/2 teaspoon paprika
- 1/2 teaspoon basil
- 1/2 teaspoon oregano
- 1 ounce sour cream
- 3 ounces Provolone cheese, freshly grated

## Nutritional Information

309 Calories
21.2g Fat
8g Total Carbs
20.4g Protein
2.6g Fiber

## Directions

Cook the cauliflower with the vegetable broth over medium-low flame until tender but crispy. Transfer the cauliflower florets to a lightly greased casserole dish.

Then, preheat your oven to 360 degrees F. In a mixing dish, thoroughly combine the scallions, garlic, milk, eggs, salt, black pepper, paprika, basil, and oregano.

Pour the scallion mixture over the cauliflower florets. Mix the sour cream and Provolone cheese; add the cheese mixture to the top. Cover with foil.

Bake in the preheated oven for about 45 minutes, until topping is lightly golden and everything is heated through.

Transfer to a cooling rack for 10 minutes before serving. Bon appétit!

# SNACKS & APPETIZERS

2 Servings 15 minutes

# 58. Skinny Cocktail Meatballs

## Ingredients

- 1/4 pound ground turkey
- 1/4 pound ground pork
- 1 ounce bacon, chopped
- 1/4 cup flaxseed meal
- 1/2 teaspoon garlic, pressed
- 1 egg, beaten
- 1/2 cup cheddar cheese, shredded
- Sea salt, to season
- 1/4 teaspoon ground black pepper
- 1/4 teaspoon cayenne pepper
- 1/4 teaspoon marjoram

## Nutritional Information

569 Calories
42.2g Fat
6.5g Total Carbs
40.1g Protein
5.7g Fiber

## Directions

Start by preheating your oven to 395 degrees F.

Thoroughly combine all ingredients in a mixing bowl. Now, form the mixture into meatballs.

Place your meatballs in a parchment-lined baking sheet. Bake in the preheated oven for about 18 minutes, rotating the pan halfway through.

Serve with toothpicks and enjoy!

# 59. Caribbean-Style Chicken Wings

2 Servings 50 minutes

## Ingredients

- 4 chicken wings
- 1 tablespoon coconut aminos
- 2 tablespoons rum
- 2 tablespoons butter
- 1 tablespoon onion powder
- 1 tablespoon garlic powder
- 1/2 teaspoon salt
- 1/4 teaspoon freshly ground black pepper
- 1/2 teaspoon red pepper flakes
- 1/4 teaspoon dried dill
- 2 tablespoons sesame seeds

## Directions

Pat dry the chicken wings. Toss the chicken wings with the remaining ingredients until well coated. Arrange the chicken wings on a parchment-lined baking sheet.

Bake in the preheated oven at 420 degrees F for 45 minutes until golden brown.

Serve with your favorite sauce for dipping. Bon appétit!

## Nutritional Information

286 Calories
18.5g Fat
5.2g Total Carbs
15.6g Protein
1.9g Fiber

2 Servings 15 minutes

# 60. Bell Pepper Boats

## Ingredients

- 2 eggs
- 1/2 red onion, chopped
- 1/2 teaspoon garlic clove, minced
- 2 ounces canned boneless sardines, drained and chopped
- 1/4 freshly ground black pepper
- 1/2 cup tomatoes, chopped
- 1/4 cup mayonnaise
- 3 tablespoons Ricotta cheese
- 3 bell peppers, deveined and halved

## Nutritional Information

371 Calories
31.1g Fat
6g Total Carbs
16.2g Protein
1.3g Fiber

## Directions

Place the eggs and water in a saucepan; bring to a rapid boil; immediately remove from the heat.

Allow it to sit, covered, for 10 minutes. Then, discard the shells, rinse the eggs under cold water, and chop them.

Thoroughly combine the onion, garlic, sardines, black pepper, tomatoes, mayonnaise, and cheese.

Stuff the pepper halves and serve well chilled. Bon appétit!

# 61. Zucchini Parmesan Chips

2 Servings 25 minutes

## Ingredients

- 1 tablespoon extra-virgin olive oil
- 1/4 teaspoon sea salt
- 1 teaspoon hot paprika
- 1/2 pound zucchini, sliced into rounds
- 2 tablespoons Parmesan cheese, grated

## Nutritional Information

52 Calories
4.6g Fat
1.4g Total Carbs
1.7g Protein
0.5g Fiber

## Directions

Gently toss the sliced zucchini with the olive oil, salt, and paprika. Place them on a tin-foil-lined baking sheet.

Sprinkle the Parmesan cheese evenly over each zucchini round.

Bake in the preheated oven at 400 degrees F for 15 to 20 minutes or until your chips turns a golden-brown color.

2 Servings 15 minutes

# 62. Ranch Kale Chips

## Ingredients

- 2 cups kale, torn into pieces
- 1 tablespoons olive oil
- Sea salt, to taste
- 1/4 teaspoon pepper
- 1/2 teaspoon onion powder
- 1/2 teaspoon garlic powder
- 1/2 teaspoon fresh dill, minced
- 1/2 tablespoon fresh parsley, minced

## Nutritional Information

68 Calories
6.6g Fat
1.4g Total Carbs
0.6g Protein
0.6g Fiber

## Directions

Start by preheating your oven to 320 degrees F.

Toss the kale leaves with all other ingredients until well coated. Bake for 10 to 14 minutes, depending on how crisp you like them.

Store the kale chips in an airtight container for up to a week. Bon appétit!

# 63. Cauliflower Bites with Asiago Cheese

2 Servings 35 minutes

## Ingredients

- 1 ½ cups cauliflower florets
- 1 tablespoon butter, softened
- 1 egg, whisked
- Sea salt and ground black pepper, to taste
- 1 teaspoon Italian seasoning mix
- 1/2 cup Asiago cheese, grated

## Nutritional Information

236 Calories
19.2g Fat
4.5g Total Carbs
12.3g Protein
1.6g Fiber

## Directions

Pulse the cauliflower in your food processor; now, heat the butter in a nonstick skillet and cook the cauliflower until golden.

Add the remaining ingredients and blend together until well incorporated.

Form the mixture into balls and flatten them with the palm of your hand. Arrange on a tinfoil-lined baking pan.

Bake in the preheated oven at 410 degrees F for 25 to 30 minutes. Serve with homemade ketchup. Bon appétit!

2 Servings

15 minutes + marinating time

# 64. Greek-Style Pork Skewers with Sauce

## Ingredients

- 1/2 pound pork loin, cut into bite-sized pieces
- 2 garlic cloves, pressed
- 1 scallion stalk, chopped
- 1/4 cup dry red wine
- 1 thyme sprig
- 1 rosemary sprig
- 1 tablespoon lemon juice
- 1 teaspoon stone ground mustard
- 1 tablespoon olive oil

**Dipping Sauce:**

- 1/2 cup Greek-style yogurt
- 1/2 teaspoon dill, ground
- 1/2 Lebanese cucumber, grated
- 1 teaspoon garlic, minced
- Sea salt, to taste
- 1/2 teaspoon ground black pepper
- 2 tablespoons cilantro leaves, roughly chopped

## Directions

Place the pork loin in a ceramic dish; add in the garlic, scallions, wine, thyme, rosemary, lemon juice, mustard, and olive oil. Let them marinate in your refrigerator for 2 to 3 hours

Thread the pork pieces onto bamboo skewers. Grill them for 5 to 6 minutes per side.

Meanwhile, whisk the remaining ingredients until well mixed. Serve the pork skewers with the sauce for dipping and enjoy!

## Nutritional Information

312 Calories
19.7g Fat
2.3g Total Carbs
29.3g Protein
0.7g Fiber

# 65. Tender Ribs with Hot Sauce

2 Servings

2 hours 10 minutes

## Ingredients

**Ribs:**

- 1 pound spare ribs
- 1 teaspoon Dijon mustard
- 1 tablespoon rice wine
- Salt and ground black pepper, to season
- 1 teaspoon garlic, pressed
- 1/2 shallot powder
- 1 teaspoon cayenne pepper
- 1/2 teaspoon ground allspice
- 1 tablespoon avocado oil

**Hot Sauce:**

- 1 teaspoon Sriracha sauce
- 1 tablespoon olive oil
- 1 cup tomato sauce, sugar-free
- 1 teaspoon garlic, minced
- Salt, to season

## Directions

Arrange the spare ribs on a parchment-lined baking pan. Add the remaining ingredients for the ribs and toss until well coated.

Bake in the preheated oven at 360 degrees F for 1 hour. Rotate the pan and roast an additional 50 to 60 minutes. Baste the ribs with the cooking liquid periodically.

In the meantime, whisk the sauce ingredients until well mixed. Pour the hot sauce over the ribs. Place under the broiler and broil for 7 to 9 minutes or until an internal temperature reaches 145 degrees F.

Brush the sauce onto each rib and serve warm. Bon appétit!

## Nutritional Information

472 Calories
27g Fat
6.5g Total Carbs
48.7g Protein
2g Fiber

2 Servings

1 hour
40 minutes

# 66. Chunky Burger Dip

## Ingredients

- 1/4 pound ground pork
- 1/4 pound ground turkey
- 1/2 red onion, chopped
- 1 garlic clove, minced
- 1 serrano pepper, chopped
- 1 bell pepper, chopped
- 2 ounces sour cream
- 1/2 cup Provolone cheese, grated
- 2 ounces tomato paste
- 1/2 teaspoon mustard
- 1/2 teaspoon dried oregano
- 1/2 teaspoon dried basil
- 1/4 teaspoon dried marjoram

## Nutritional Information

423 Calories
29g Fat
5g Total Carbs
32.1g Protein
1g Fiber

## Directions

Place all of the above ingredients, except for the sour cream and Provolone cheese in your slow cooker.

Cook for 1 hour 30 minutes at Low setting. Afterwards, fold in sour cream and cheese.

Serve warm with celery sticks if desired. Bon appétit!

# DESSERTS

2 Servings 25 minutes

# 67. Chocolate and Coconut Fudge Brownies

## Ingredients

- 2 tablespoons ground flax
- 1/4 cup coconut flour
- 1/4 teaspoon baking powder
- 1/4 teaspoon cinnamon
- 1/4 teaspoon cardamom
- 2 tablespoons cocoa powder
- 1/3 cup xylitol
- 1 tablespoon dark rum
- 1/4 cup coconut oil
- 1 egg, beaten
- 1 ounce sugar-free dark chocolate, melted
- 1/4 teaspoon coconut extract

## Nutritional Information

405 Calories
40g Fat
8.8g Total Carbs
6.3g Protein
5.3g Fiber

## Directions

Mix the ground flax, coconut flour, baking powder, cinnamon, cardamom, cocoa powder, and xylitol in a mixing bowl. In another mixing bowl, mix the remaining ingredients until everything is well combined.

Add the wet mixture to the dry mixture; mix to combine well. Spoon the batter in a lightly greased baking pan.

Bake in the preheated oven at 360 degrees F for 18 to 20 minutes or until a tester comes out dry and clean. Bon appétit!

# 68. Favorite Chocolate Crepes

2 Servings 40 minutes

## Ingredients

- 1/2 cup coconut flour
- 1/2 teaspoon baking soda
- A pinch of salt
- 2 tablespoons monk fruit powder
- 1 tablespoon unsweetened cocoa powder
- 1/4 teaspoon ground cinnamon
- 1/4 teaspoon ground cloves
- 2 egg, beaten
- 1/4 cup coconut milk, unsweetened
- 1/2 teaspoon vanilla
- 2 tablespoons coconut oil, melted

## Nutritional Information

330 Calories
31.9g Fat
7.1g Total Carbs
7.3g Protein
3.5g Fiber

## Directions

In a mixing dish, thoroughly combine the coconut flour, baking soda, salt, monk fruit, cocoa powder, cinnamon, and cloves.

In a separate dish, whisk the eggs with the coconut milk and vanilla until frothy. Add the egg mixture to the coconut flour mixture. Set aside for 20 to 30 minutes to rest.

Heat up 1 tablespoon of the coconut oil in a nonstick frying pan over medium-high flame. Spoon 1/2 of the prepared batter into the pan. Cook for 2 minutes per side until they are cooked in the middle.

Melt another tablespoon of the coconut oil. Repeat with the remaining batter. Serve with your favorite filling such as cream cheese, butter, shredded coconut or unsweetened jam. Bon appétit!

2 Servings

1 hour
10 minutes

# 69. Classic Blueberry Cheesecake

## Ingredients

**Crust:**

- 4 tablespoons butter, room temperature
- 1/4 teaspoon ground star anise
- 1/2 cup almond flour

**Filling:**

- 1/4 cup coconut-milk yogurt
- 4 ounces ricotta cheese, at room temperature
- 1/3 cup xylitol
- 1/2 teaspoon vanilla paste
- 2 eggs, whisked
- A handful of fresh blueberries

## Nutritional Information

598 Calories
58.9g Fat
7.4g Total Carbs
13.3g Protein
2g Fiber

## Directions

In a mixing bowl, thoroughly combine all of the crust ingredients.

Then, scrape the mixture into a lightly greased baking pan; place in your freezer for 30 minutes.

Then, mix the coconut-milk yogurt, ricotta cheese, xylitol, and vanilla using an electric mixer. Now, fold in the eggs, one at a time, mixing continuously until well blended. Pour the filling over the prepared crust.

Bake in the preheated oven at 450 degrees F for 10 minutes; reduce temperature to 360 degrees F and bake an additional 30 minutes.

Serve well chilled, garnished with fresh blueberries. Enjoy!

# 70. Flourless Almond Butter Cookies

2 Servings 20 minutes

## Ingredients

- 2 tablespoons coconut flour
- 1/3 cup almond butter, at room temperature
- A pinch of salt
- A pinch of grated nutmeg
- 1/3 cup monk fruit powder
- 1/2 teaspoon vanilla essence
- 1/4 teaspoon cinnamon
- 1 egg, whisked

## Nutritional Information

316 Calories
27g Fat
9.1g Total Carbs
11.1g Protein
5.3g Fiber

## Directions

Start by preheating your oven to 345 degrees F.

Mix all of the above ingredients until everything is well combined.

Shape the batter into balls and flatten them with the palm of your hand. Arrange your cookies on a tinfoil-lined baking sheet.

Bake in the preheated oven approximately 16 minutes until golden colored. Bon appétit!

2 Servings

10 minutes

# 71. Nutty Cheesecakes Bowls

## Ingredients

- 1/2 cup double cream
- 2 ounces mascarpone cheese, at room temperature
- 1 teaspoon liquid Stevia
- 1/2 teaspoon vanilla extract
- 2 heaping tablespoons smooth peanut butter

## Nutritional Information

233 Calories
19.2g Fat
6g Total Carbs
6.8g Protein
0.9g Fiber

## Directions

Whip the double cream, cheese, and Stevia until creamy and uniform.

Now, stir in the vanilla and continue mixing for a minute more.

Divide the mixture between serving bowls; top each bowl with a teaspoon of peanut butter and serve well chilled.

# 72. Creamy Almond Bars

2 Servings 40 minutes

## Ingredients

**First Layer:**

- 1 egg, beaten
- 2 tablespoons coconut oil, at room temperature
- 1/8 teaspoon ground cinnamon
- 1/8 teaspoon ground cardamom
- 4 tablespoons monk fruit powder
- 1/4 cup flax meal
- 1/4 cup coconut flour

**Second Layer:**

- 1 ounce Greek-style yogurt
- 3 ounces cream cheese
- 4 tablespoons monk fruit powder

**Topping:**

- 1/4 cup almonds, chopped

## Nutritional Information

509 Calories
48g Fat
8.4g Total Carbs
13.2g Protein
3.9g Fiber

## Directions

Thoroughly combine all ingredients for the first layer. Press the crust into a parchment-lined baking pan.

Then, mix the Greek yogurt with the cream cheese and monk fruit. Spread this mixture over the crust using a wide spatula.

Bake in the preheated oven at 360 degrees F for 20 to 25 minutes. Place on a cooling rack for 10 to 15 minutes and then, transfer to your refrigerator.

Top with chopped almonds and serve well chilled. Bon appétit!

2 Servings 30 minutes

# 73. Chocolate Chip Blondies

## Ingredients

- 1/2 cup almond flour
- 1/4 teaspoon cream of tartar
- 1/4 teaspoon baking soda
- A pinch of salt
- A pinch of grated nutmeg
- 1 egg, whisked
- 1/4 cup butter, melted
- 1 tablespoon milk
- 1/2 cup Swerve sweetener
- 1/2 teaspoon vanilla bean seeds
- 1/4 cup chocolate chips, unsweetened

## Nutritional Information

347 Calories
34g Fat
5.2g Total Carbs
5.7g Protein
2.8g Fiber

## Directions

In a mixing bowl, thoroughly combine the almond flour, cream of tartar, baking soda, salt, and nutmeg. In another bowl, whisk the egg, butter, milk, and sweetener.

Add the almond flour mixture to the egg mixture and mix to combine well. Afterwards, stir in the vanilla bean seeds and chocolate chips; stir again using a spatula.

Scrape the batter into a parchment-lined baking pan. Bake in the preheated oven at 360 degrees F for 22 to 25 minutes. Don't over-bake, the blondies should remain juicy in the center.

Let it cool down; then, cut into equal size squares and enjoy!

# 74. Classic Chocolate Mousse

2 Servings

5 minutes + chilling time

## Ingredients

- 4 tablespoons unsweetened cocoa powder
- 1/4 teaspoon vanilla essence
- 1/4 teaspoon rum extract
- 1/8 teaspoon ground cardamom
- 1/8 teaspoon grated nutmeg
- 4 tablespoons almond milk
- 2 ounces cream cheese
- 1/2 ripe avocado, pitted and peeled
- 1/4 cup swerve sweetener

## Nutritional Information

163 Calories
14.6g Fat
9.8g Total Carbs
4.7g Protein
5.9g Fiber

## Directions

Simply throw all ingredients into the bowl of your blender or a food processor.

Blend until everything is creamy and well incorporated.

Spoon into two dessert bowls. Serve well chilled. Bon appétit!

2 Servings

10 minutes

# 75. Pecan Pie Chocolate Truffles

## Ingredients

- 2 tablespoons coconut oil
- 1/4 cup coconut butter
- A pinch of salt
- A pinch of grated nutmeg
- 1/4 teaspoon ground cinnamon
- 3 tablespoons cocoa powder
- 1 teaspoon liquid Stevia
- 1/4 cup pecans, ground

## Directions

In a mixing bowl, thoroughly combine all ingredients until everything is well blended and incorporated.

Scrape the batter into candy molds and keep in your freezer. Bon appétit!

## Nutritional Information

436 Calories
47.6g Fat
6.9g Total Carbs
3.4g Protein
4.5g Fiber

60523985R00057

Made in the USA
Middletown, DE
15 August 2019